JOHN R. HARRIS ARCHITECTS

JOHN R. HARRIS ARCHITECTS

A.E.J. Morris

DipArch (UCL) DiplTP(Lond) ARIBA FRGS

Hurtwood Press

Published by Hurtwood Press Ltd.
London Road, Westerham, Kent

First Published 1984

© John R. Harris Architects 1984

ISBN 0 903696 28 2

Designed by A.E.J. Morris

Photographs in the book were taken by the following:
Robert Belton, D.I.C. Studios, David Dunstan, John R.
Harris, Rosina Harris, W. Mark Harris, Yves Kerihuel,
John Lawrence, Ron Margetson, Christopher Mitchell,
A.E.J. Morris, Sydney Newbery, Brian Redfern, Henk
Snoek, Graham Solano, Richard Turpin.

Set in Monotype Plantin series 110

Printed in Great Britain by Westerham Press Ltd.

Foreword

War parts and it binds. It flung us both into the Tropics; John as a prisoner-of-war to Hong Kong; and me as a Royal Engineer to West Africa; and for us both there was time enough to contemplate and to absorb the varied effects of climate on man and his buildings.

We both married students from the Architectural Association and lived to celebrate long years of work together contributing each in our own way to the creation of an architecture fit for its purpose and good in itself.

There these similarities may rest for John's story goes on longer and continues.

There is in the lives of successful men a moment when they assume power over their chosen vocation and his came when he won the open competition for the State Hospital in Doha, the Capital of Qatar in the Arabian Gulf with a design that was the model for a hospital in the dry tropics and the prototype of all such hospitals to come.

As architects make their statements and prove their worth by works, so this hospital, with its sensitive reaction to the effects of climate and its loving care for its patients, standing there after thirty years service in prime condition, was the foundation of a practice that expanded by personal recommendation and the acquired skill to meet further competition from wherever it came.

Corbusier once said to me that there was more talent in the world than character to match it, and surely John's accumulation of fine works in many parts of the world, speaks of a resolution and a dedication rare even among the best of architects, recalling another of Corbusier's sayings appropriate to the widespread activities of John's firms as architects, planners and directors of great urban affairs – "there is no such thing as detail: all is important".

In the pages that follow will be found the fine record of one who built more hospitals than could be thought possible in a lifespan, and many other works in other spheres beside, none finer than the Dubai International Trade Centre on which he paid his quite most graceful tribute to architecture.

I pay my respects to a grand architect and friend and for the rest what follows speaks more eloquently than I.

E. Maxwell Fry CBE RA FRIBA
March 1984

24 Devonshire Place, London; the main office since 1963.
Left a group of views, including the courtyard garden around which the offices are planned.
Right a plan perspective relating the original Devonshire Place building of the 1780s (top) and the firm's new office building fronting onto Marylebone High Street, with the linking gallery along the central courtyard.

Contents

John and Jill Harris with Stuart Aston, who became a partner in 1973, drew out the competition in their Queen Anne Street office in London.

The State Hospital at Doha was the first major international architectural competition for a hospital to be held since before World War II. It attracted a total of 335 entries from around the world. John Harris's success was to have two far-reaching effects on the nature of the future work of the practice: first, it was the beginning of an international health-care building specialisation around which their other varied work has developed and secondly, the geographical location of Doha led naturally to John R. Harris becoming established in the Arabian Gulf long before the oil-financed building boom occurred.

They were among the very first architects to be working in the Gulf and it can be no exaggeration to claim on their behalf that this book amounts in considerable part to a history of modern architecture in the region. John Harris's reminiscences of 'thirty years in the Gulf' would make a fascinating separate book, with architecture forming

only an essential central focus of wide-ranging personal experiences of the eventful period in history that has seen desert communities transposed into still-growing, international cities.

The unusual origins of the practice through the Doha competition success enabled John R. Harris to become established on the international scene at a time when comparable opportunities for other British practices to work overseas were few. This, however, is one of the reasons why the firm is far less well known in British architectural circles than is deserved by the quality and variety of their work. In addition, until the recent changes in the Royal Institute of British Architects' policy on practice promotion, John Harris preferred to rely primarily on the firm's reputation with established clients.

The Doha competition was to be not only of great significance as

Tuen Mun Hospital, Hong Kong; an early design sketch showing the general form of the 1,606-bed district general hospital, designed with the Architectural Office, Building Development Department, Hong Kong Government.

PART ONE

Hong Kong: a circle closes....

After the fall of Hong Kong to the Japanese on Christmas Day 1941, John Harris, then a 22-year-old British Army lieutenant, much to his amazement, found himself still alive. The ensuing four years of captivity taught many lessons and provided the erstwhile architectural student with an invaluable – if not then fully appreciated – practical introduction to the basic principles of tropical design and construction.

Forty years on as the latest of several such coincidences which have occurred during his subsequent architectural career, John Harris in 1981 returned to Hong Kong at the invitation of the Hong Kong Government as principal partner in the broad-based international practice of John R. Harris Architects. This time, however, to be commissioned to work with the Public Works Department as architects for Hong Kong's major new 1,600-bed Tuen Mun Hospital.

As if it were not already an extraordinary twist of fate to return to the place he had for so long doubted ever being able to leave alive; as a further appointment some months later, he was then asked to prepare plans for extending the existing St Teresa's Hospital over the very same Argyle Street prison camp, the original huts of which were still standing! The Tuen Mun Hospital contract was won in the face of strong international architectural competition, and as such provides an introductory measure of the firm's successes during the intervening decades.

The first thirty years....

Although formally established in the autumn of 1950, the international practice dates effectively from three years later, when in September 1953, John Harris, then in practice with his wife, Jill Rowe, was awarded first premium in the Royal Institute of British Architects' international competition for the design of a new State Hospital in Doha, the capital of the State of Qatar on the Arabian Gulf. Later that month, the Ruler, His Highness Sheikh Ali Bin Abdullah Bin Jasmin Al-Thani, KBE, gave his instructions to proceed with the detailed design and construction of the new hospital.

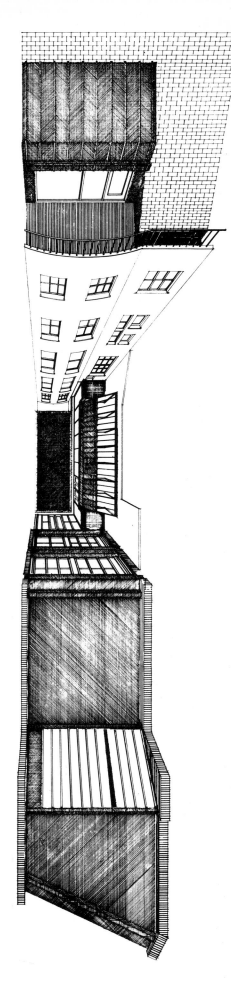

the founding opportunity for the future world-wide practice: more immediately it was the salvation of the small office which the Harris's had set up three years earlier. With great difficulty they had been able to keep their practice running during that hard postwar period in Britain of building licensing and materials shortages. The Doha competition could well have been their last endeavour.

John Harris: Hong Kong to the Arabian Gulf. . . .

John Harris joined the Architectural Association School in London in 1937. His studies were interrupted by war service, initially in the United Kingdom and then from September 8th 1940 in Hong Kong. Since then, September 8th has always been a date of extra-special personal significance: it was on that day in 1945 that he was to leave Hong Kong after its liberation, and in London on September 8th 1953 the news of the Doha competition success was announced.

Involvement in the architecture of health-care buildings dates back to the summer of 1935 when at the age of 16, he went on a study tour of Scandinavian hospitals with his father, Alfred Harris, who was

Tuen Mun Hospital; part plan of the 11-storey wards block, drawn by the firm's computer facility; and a photograph of the model.

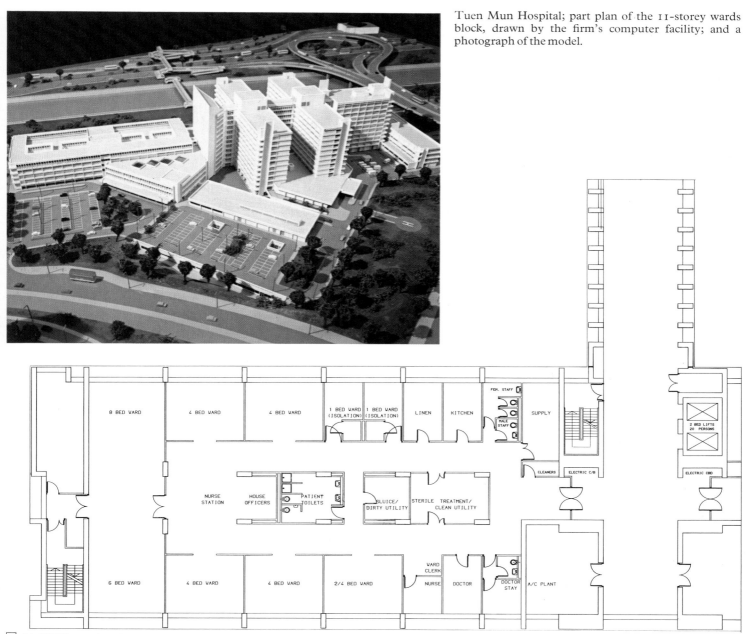

File #>TUEMUN >HK   Plot scale 1:2.500 Generated 30 SEP 82 15.09.10
Drawing HK2   Plot no 5 Issue 1
Extent X1210.0/Y144.0 to X2372.0/Y1184.0 (MM)

the surveyor for the rebuilding of Westminster Hospital, and the hospital's architect, Lionel Pearson of Adams, Holden and Pearson. It is recalled how Lionel Pearson's inventive planning of the Westminster's kitchens and dining rooms at roof level was to provide a precedent for the design of the New Dubai Hospital completed in 1982.

Prewar the first two years at the A.A. School were completed before, as a Territorial Army volunteer of one year's standing, John Harris was called up in September 1939. Commissioned in the summer of 1940, his posting was to Hong Kong where for more than 3½ years, after Christmas 1941, he was held in various prison camps. During that time Lieutenant Harris played an active, highly secret role with the British Army Aid Group in South China. Surviving that experience, the recollection is savoured of first re-encountering the British traditions of 'pink gin' and a copy of *Country Life* – with its pictures of unbelievably distant villages and farmsteads – in the wardroom of H.M.S. Belfast, one of the first Royal Navy warships to return to Hong Kong. Now permanently moored in the Pool of London, that same wardroom provided a sentimentally appropriate venue for a London office party.

The first letter sent home after release in September 1945 had requested registration back at the A.A. School at the earliest opportunity; studying there was resumed in January 1946, this time in the company of a fellow student, his future wife Jill. John Harris's success story has been based not only on exceptional ability to make the most of the chances and half-chances that come an architect's way, but also through identification of possible openings before they actually materialise, thereby managing to be on hand at the right moment. Mere 'luck' – as held responsible by so many others for success or failure – has been denied the controlling role in his life.

Thoughtful preparation is exemplified by John Harris's choice of a final year student thesis project, which in the context of subsequent major commissions, might otherwise be thought to have been on the seemingly inappropriate subject of 'farm buildings'.

Why farm buildings? 'Because', it is explained, 'I realised that in the extraordinary difficult postwar economic period, farm buildings were the only development exempt from restrictions imposed on almost any other form of construction. They represented one of the very few ways open to an architect to get started.' Farm buildings at the time were also 'in great need of architectural thought, and presented a challenge in the design field, in particular with the immediate postwar emphasis on prefabrication techniques.'

Even farm buildings, though, had to be in the future for a while, because the first year or so out of the A.A. School was to be spent in completing his RIBA qualification, drawing up the final design of the Chapel at Downing College, Cambridge, by Sir Herbert Baker, of the firm of Sir Herbert Baker and Scott. In June 1950, John and Jill Harris were married and in the following November, in architectural practice, they opened their first office at 40 George Street in London's Marylebone district, where with two subsequent moves John R. Harris Architects have remained based ever since. The present main office at 24 Devonshire Place, is illustrated at the front of the book. The first office in George Street was in one half of one room above a shop designed by James Cubitt. It was heated by an oil stove and tea was made with an electric kettle on the floor. There was one shared telephone instrument.

The London Transport Headquarters Building, St James's, designed by Dr Holden; drawn by John Harris in a Japanese prison camp and tinted with the limited materials available.

4

Specialisation in farm buildings proved to have been worthwhile, but only just. One particular commission near Bagshot in Surrey is remembered with pleasure, and that type of work with such conversions, extensions and war-damage repairs as came their way, kept the two of them occupied but without ever fully covering the rent. Nevertheless there was independence, time, and above all *incentive* to work on architectural competitions. While still at the A.A. School, they had entered the Guildford Town Hall competition, gaining an honourable mention. The winning scheme was never built, prompting the comment, expressed with a depth of feeling derived from comparable personal disappointments: 'the poor architects who won then had the tragedy of gaining the premium without ever seeing their design realised.' In practice together, the Nairobi Town Hall competition was attempted in 1951 without success. Then with work running out and prospects gloomy, preparations were made in 1952 for entering the Doha State Hospital competition.

A commitment to the competition system as a means of obtaining commissions and gaining experience beyond the bounds of everyday practice has been characteristic of the work of the practice. This continues to involve participation in open architectural design competitions, such as that for the Doha State Hospital; limited design competition against other similarly nominated architects; and competition against known or unknown architectural rivals on the basis of past work and professional repute, as evidenced by submissions of examples of relevant work and details of experience. In recent years the latter two categories have become commonplace on the international scene. A further related requirement experienced by the firm is the need to carry out work on major overseas projects on the basis of membership of a multi-disciplinary consultants consortium, in which there have been numerous involvements during the three decades of practice.

The State Hospital, Doha

In 1952 there were two major RIBA competitions: one at Doha for the State Hospital and the other, more famous, for Coventry Cathedral won by Sir Basil Spence. The question has not been taken up, but the Doha competition was clearly recognised by John Harris as the more worthwhile challenge. It was three times larger than Coventry and led to the foundation of modern medical services in the Southern Gulf. (As a matter of interest it was the last RIBA open competition held in the Arab world.)

In entering for the Doha competition John Harris had two personal advantages. First, he had developed a feel for climate, having experienced those years in Hong Kong without air-conditioning, or fans, and all the other aids to comfortable present day life in hot climates. Secondly, he had already made a first visit to the Arabian Gulf in 1951 in connection with the design of the Kuwait Building Research Laboratories.

In the glaring light of that firsthand experience, the planning and elevational detailing of the State Hospital design was largely determined by the inter-related requirements of solar control and natural ventilation, the success of which was recognised by the assessor, Alexander S. Gray, FRIBA, who reported: 'I have no hesitation in awarding first place to design number 58. Of all the designs submitted this offers the best solution to the problem. The ward units are

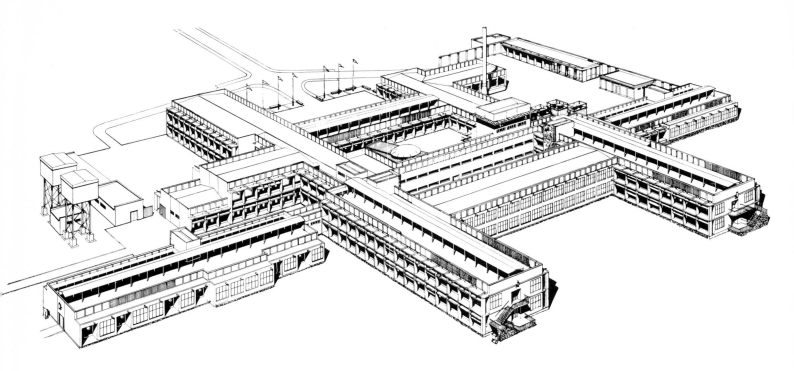

particularly well planned to afford good supervision and economy in working, while they are sufficiently compact for air-conditioning without detriment to good cross-ventilation. The planning of the single-bed wards to avoid sun and glare is ingenious . . .' (This particular use of reflected sunlight has subsequently been adopted by other architects in many parts of the world.)

It was Bill Spragg, then secretary of the RIBA, who telephoned during the morning of September 8th, 1953 with the news that Mr Hugh Hale, the State Engineer to the Government of Qatar, was in London and would like to meet the architect that day for lunch. Mr Hale's first remark was to suggest that John Harris should depart forthwith for Qatar: 'I wish you to encounter the heat of the Gulf before it cools. You will leave in four days time.' So out he went, never thinking that his total flights to the Gulf alone would have exceeded 200 by the summer of 1983.

His Highness, Sheikh Ali, the Ruler of Qatar, was somewhat taken aback at the evident youthfulness of his architect. He was curious to know why more time was needed to complete the working drawings for the new hospital. His own new Palace, he explained, had been marked out on the sand and work had started as soon as he had given his authority. His people, he added, had been waiting for over a year for their new hospital, which was to replace the existing small American Mission Hospital of some ten beds and provide the nucleus of Qatar's first full medical service. It was at that time that the first significant oil revenues were becoming available to the State of Qatar.

John Harris, with quick thinking, produced the acceptable answer whereby a separate foundation contract would enable work to start on site within the following six weeks. The nine months required for preparation of final working drawings and contract documents could then run in parallel with the evident progress on site. The use of a separate foundations contract was subsequently to become a characteristic of major project construction in the Middle East, where speed is often a prime factor.

Details of the systems of solar control and natural ventilation are described below as also is the significance of the State Hospital in the history of modern architecture in the Arabian Gulf, where amongst other innovations, it saw the introduction of the first passenger elevator, and the first use of prestressed concrete, in the southern Gulf region. It is important to note that after more than a quarter of a century's hard service, the 'old' State Hospital – renamed the Rumaillah Hospital – required only redecoration and upgrading of service installations and related non-structural repairs, to look forward to a new lease of life for post-operative recuperation. A salutory reminder of the fact that by no means all of the early modern buildings in the Arabian Gulf have either already undergone serious failure, or can be expected to be of only limited useful life.

Above the State Hospital, Doha; an aerial photograph at completion stage, showing the new building in its then edge-of-town desert location.
Below two views of the hospital's matured landscape planting;
right at the end of one of the main block wings;
left across one of the interior courtyards.

A broad-based international practice

As related earlier, John Harris received his first overseas appointment in Kuwait in 1952. The commission was for the design of new Building Research Laboratories in that country, as proposed by Mr R. Fitzmaurice, a senior member of staff at the Building Research Station at Watford, England. Over the years, the Kuwait Laboratories have been responsible for an extensive programme of research into the uses of buildings materials in hot, dry climates, leading to great improvements in the design and detailing of construction projects in the Arabian Gulf and in many other similar parts of the world.

In London, from September 1953, final design and detailing of the Doha State Hospital kept the small practice in Queen Anne Street fully occupied for some nine months. Subsequently it grew slowly but steadily with general U.K. commissions providing diversity to the work. In 1956, with the national programme of health service building beginning to gain momentum, John R. Harris Architects were awarded their first British hospital project, that of carrying out an extensive programme of alterations to Heatherwood Hospital at Ascot, Surrey.

Since then the firm has been engaged on a number of hospitals and related projects in the U.K., including the development plan for the Royal Northern Hospital, London; the new Ealing District Hospital, Middlesex; and the redevelopment plan for Stoke Mandeville Hospital, near Aylesbury, Buckinghamshire. In addition, there has been work at King Edward VII Hospital, Windsor; and Upper Heyford Hospital and Bentwaters Medical Centre have been built for the Property Services Agency. The firm has been the architects for major health-care development in sixteen countries.

The period 1953 to 1958 saw the beginning of large-scale urban development in the Lower Gulf and, in 1958, John Harris was invited by the Ruler, His Highness Sheikh Rashid Ibn Said Al-Maktoum, to visit Dubai in order to prepare a first Town Plan for the City. Although a long established, prosperous commercial port, Dubai by the late 1950s lacked modern harbour facilities. The creek itself had silted up such that only shallow draft ships could enter to discharge their cargoes, and it was known that a new deep-water harbour was necessary in order to ensure Dubai's increasing prosperity. Accordingly, the Town Plan was drawn up at a critical moment in Dubai's history, before the construction boom of the succeeding decades. Sheikh Rashid himself was personally involved in considering the main aspects of the Plan preparation. A major review of the development plan was carried out by the Practice in 1971.

John Harris's first building commission in Dubai was for the Al-Maktoum Hospital. In 1958 this was only a single shed-like structure containing eight beds, with a small X-ray unit and one operating theatre. Nevertheless, run almost single-handed by Dr McCawley, the hospital was a haven for medical treatment for many thousands of square miles around. During the following ten years, with scarce building resources and at a total cost of about £180,000, John Harris, with Sheikh Rashid's guidance, extended the hospital, ward by ward, to a total of 125 beds.

Subsequently, with benefit of Dubai's greatly increased wealth, the Practice has been responsible for the design of a further five major new hospitals in the City, the most recently completed of which is the prestigious Dubai Hospital, an acute general hospital with 638 beds. This commission was won in an International Architectural Design

The Roman Catholic Church, Ruwi, Muscat, Oman; the church in a new district of the Capital City of Oman was designed for a congregation of 250 people.

The Meeting Hall, Shell Recreation Centre, Seria, Negara Brunei Darussalam.

8

Competition. On completion in the summer of 1982, the Dubai Hospital has been recognised as one of the most advanced in the world. The Practice has maintained an office in Dubai since 1958; latterly located in the 39-storey Trade Centre Tower, designed for Sheikh Rashid in 1975.

At the northern end of the Gulf, an office in Kuwait has been maintained, according to local commitments, with the Headquarters base for the Kuwait Navy their most recent project. It was from Kuwait, in 1955, that John Harris became one of the first Britons to return to the great oil refinery at Abadan, after its take-over by Iran in 1952, crossing the Shatt al Arab river secretly in a small dhow. For some years after, the firm was involved in the rehabilitation of several thousand houses for the National Iranian Oil Company. At the same time, Maxwell Fry and Jane Drew were responsible for similar architectural work in the oil fields. An office was opened in Tehran in 1957, with a continuous programme of work carried out for NIOC. Recent

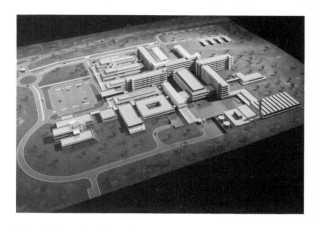

The University Teaching Hospital, Tripoli, Libya; a 600-bed hospital.

Abbotabad General Hospital, Pakistan; a project for 1,500 beds, with staff accomodation and recreational and leisure facilities.

projects in Iran were the design of the Christian Hospital at Isfahan, and alterations to the hospital at Shiraz, both in 1979.

In addition to Qatar and Dubai, the third country in which John Harris has been most involved is Oman, where the commission to design the Ottoman Bank building in Muscat was received in March 1966. On a prominent site adjoining the main gateway into the old walled city, this building, designed by Michael Foster, is a successful instance of architecture which is not only unmistakably of its time, but also which is respectful of its cultural context: an aspect of the international work of the firm which is returned to below. In August 1966, The Sultan extended an invitation to discuss participation in a programme of town planning and Government buildings, and this has continued to the present day. The main office of John R. Harris Associates in Muscat is now a diversified general practice in Oman, having its own important branch office at Salalah.

The Christian Mission Hospital, Isfahan, Iran.

9

Elsewhere in the Middle East, John R. Harris Architects were responsible for the first development plan in 1961 for Abu Dhabi, on which basis the modern city has developed. In Abu Dhabi the firm has designed both the British Embassy, and the United States Ambassador's residences. In Bahrain there has been Bank and Hotel work, and in Sharjah (one of the other United Arab Emirates, adjoining Dubai) they were invited to design a new polo ground complex. This subsequently served as an introduction to a comparable project, and related work, in Brunei. One other Middle East project is the design for a 600-bed hospital for Tripoli, Libya.

The office in Brunei was opened in 1976, in connection with work for the Royal Brunei Polo Club, including the construction of a park and a lake, a grass farm and a rice mill. The first architects' office was a simple raised structure, of a traditional vernacular character, superbly situated alongside the South China Sea. This little building

Below the firm's site office designed for the construction of the Royal Brunei Polo Club. This building was subsequently retained by His Majesty The Sultan.
Bottom 25 Rue de la Victoire, Paris; office refurbishment and conversion, with Courbe and Duboz, for the Legal and General Assurance Society.
Left the Dubai International Trade Centre; the 39-storey office tower is the tallest building in the Arab world, from the top of which can be seen five States of the United Arab Emirates.

so impressed His Highness The Sultan that he requested it to be retained for his own use.

There are four further international projects of importance: the new 700-bed University of Maiduguri Teaching Hospital in Nigeria; the extensive up-grading of the 1,200 bed Bahawalpur Hospital in Pakistan; hotel design in Sardinia; and architectural consultancy work for the new 1,200 bed Kuala Lumpur General Hospital.

In conclusion, rounding out the international basis of the firm an office has been opened in Hong Kong for the 1600-bed Tuen Mun Hospital and other work.

In Europe, John R. Harris has been in partnership with Courbe et Duboz from 1976, engaged in a programme of city centre commercial projects in Antwerp, Brussels, Lille, Strasbourg and Paris. John Harris himself was elected a member of L'Ordre des Architectes Français in 1978 and the firm maintains an office in Paris.

Al Baha Sports Centre, Kingdom of Saudi Arabia; designed to serve the region of Al Baha, south of Taif in the south-west of the Kingdom, the facilities include swimming and diving pools, and gymnasia – all to Olympic standards. There is also a floodlit stadium for Association Football and athletics. The complex contains a mosque, administrative centre, a large theatre, and residential accommodation.

The site plan reproduced below is from a colour computer plot drawn by the JRHA CAAD facility.

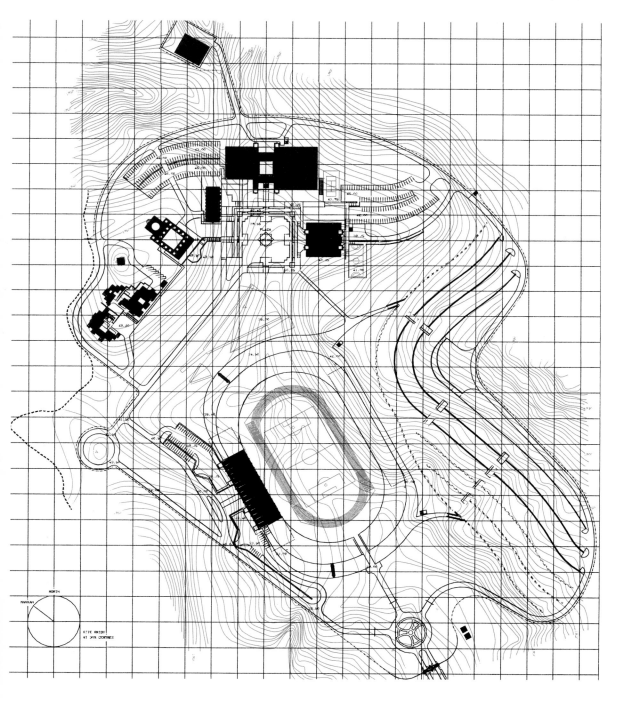

The architecture: underlying themes

As a not unusual enduring effect of formative early experiences, the construction of the Doha State Hospital ingrained – a deliberate, and under those exceptionally demanding circumstances an entirely appropriate play on words – a number of fundamental architectural values. In combination and as necessarily modified from time to time, they have come to provide the essential architectural philosophy of John R. Harris Architects. The most noteworthy of these values (or themes) are described and illustrated as the basis of this further general introductory first part of the book; summarised without sequential significance, they are as follows:

– an overriding preference for simple, uncomplicated detailing and related methods of construction; relying on proven techniques and materials, with an emphasis on the traditional methods – but only where architecturally appropriate. It would be entirely misleading at the outset to imply that respect of traditional values necessarily results only in 'old-fashioned' buildings. A glance through the range of work illustrated can but serve to establish otherwise;

Thorney Court Apartments, Palace Gate, London; a detail view of brickwork at the south-west corner, showing the use of special bricks at the angles, and the sills and reveals of window openings.

– the *vital* necessity of designing in sympathy with local climatic conditions and within local economic constraints: a consideration of paramount importance in those seemingly long past Gulf days (and nights) before air-conditioning; the relevance of which, moreover, can but continue to prevail in those numerous economically disadvantaged 'Third World' countries where Western architectural expertise, properly applied, has so much yet to contribute;

– a deeply rooted regard for quietly well-mannered, good-neighbourly architecture that respects not only its immediate physical surroundings, but also its cultural context: an architectural approach which has been responsible for what amounts to more than JRHA's fair share of the outstanding modern buildings in the Gulf and elsewhere.

– the need to pay full and proper attention to the ground surfaces around and within buildings, both as the visual extension of architectural forms, and also as a means whereby significant microclimatic improvements can be effected. In addition, importance is given to the use of planting for enhancement of interior lighting conditions;

– last, but in the business of architecture by far the most significant, there is a constant endeavour to provide a highly professional service to clients, often under unusually demanding circumstances; the continuing success of which is evidenced by the pleasingly high proportion of subsequent further commissions from satisfied clients.

In addition to description of these main themes underlying the work; summary consideration is given to the work of John R. Harris Architects in the fields of competitions; interiors; and the conversion and refurbishment of existing buildings.

Al Nahda Hospital, Muscat, Oman; the Nurses Hostel (left) and Doctors Flats (right) exemplifying the use of painted, rendered concrete blockwork as external wall surfaces, with the contrasting visual relief of louvre windows and shutters, and roof screening.

Building from first principles

Apocryphal or not, the attitude implied by Frank Lloyd Wright's return telegram: 'move your chair', to the client who complained where his roof was leaking, could never knowingly be attributed to the Harris offices. Allowing that things can but occasionally go wrong, given such a large architectural output; their response would take the form of someone suitably senior on the motorway, or the first available flight, not only to put it right as soon as possible, but also to find out how it had happened in the first place, in order to avoid recurrence. 'Prevention is better than cure', could well be pinned up over their drawing-boards, and the corollary: 'a problem avoided is a detail solved', could well serve as John Harris's personal architectural motto.

Whatever the contribution of the Doha experience (and more than likely its main effect was to consolidate existing architectural values), from then on, the buildings are characteristically notable for their straightforward, economic planning; uncomplicated 'first principles' detailing; and reliance generally, but by no means always, on traditional methods of construction.

However *notable* these attributes, they have all too seldom been those of the *noticeable* buildings of recent decades. Neither has the firm's architecturally 'eye-catching' competition and other work of recent years been accorded its fair share of attention, mainly because of its widely international origins.

Facing brickwork has been a first-choice elevational material in 96 Britain, with Thorney Court apartment building a particularly good example of its use for an important site facing Kensington Palace Gardens in London. Other notable brick architecture illustrated in the book includes the seaside flats and commercial development at 47 Worthing, and Park Hospital, near Nottingham, designed for a sensitive landscape location. Exceptionally, abroad, it was possible to 16 import bricks from Iran, across the Gulf, into Dubai for a residence.

For major international projects, where a more appropriate elevational finish than rendered blockwork is possible, within budget, materials used have included marble, for a number of buildings; ceramic mosaic tiles, as for Tuen Mun Hospital, Hong Kong; improved surface coatings in a number of instances; and precast concrete, as detailed with great effect for sun-shade elevational screen 18 components on the Dubai Trade Centre Tower; perimeter columns and panels of the adjoining Hilton Hotel; and horizontal undersill and access balcony panels on Government Buildings in The Sultanate of Oman.

Other than in the design of a number of competition entries, there have been but limited relevant opportunities for use of what have become known as 'high-technology' materials and construction 46 methods. Examples illustrated include the services block for Stoke Mandeville Hospital, an appropriate exercise in curtain-walling, reflecting the main hospital building which was designed by the practice using the 'Oxford Method' of lightweight system building.

Above a Mosque in Kuwait; traditional joinery detailing of timber screen and doors.
Below the University of Maiduguri Teaching Hospital, Nigeria; shown at an advanced stage of construction. The 600-bed hospital is mainly of economic, single-storey insitu concrete frame construction, with concrete block infilling. Need for natural ventilation was a primary determinant of the architectural planning.

Left Thorney Court Apartments, London; seen across Kensington Palace Gardens.
Below Stoke Mandeville Hospital, near Aylesbury, England; the main hospital block constructed using the 'Oxford Method' of industrialised system building, seen through the metal and glass curtain walling of the boiler house.
Bottom a commercial development of shops and seaside flats at Worthing, England; the building second from left, designed in facing brickwork on the seafront.

15

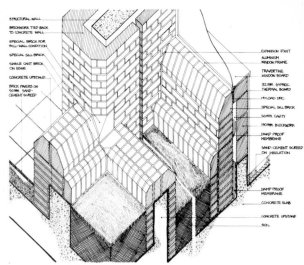

Two brickwork studies illustrating uses in combination of special facing bricks.

Government Administration Building, Oman; vertical ribbed finish, precast concrete cladding components facing an insitu concrete structural frame.

A Banker's Residence, Dubai; facing bricks imported across the Gulf from Iran, combined with projecting, sun-shading rendered concrete first floor balconies and roof terrace.

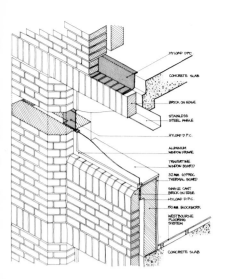
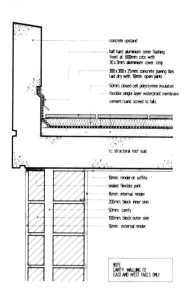
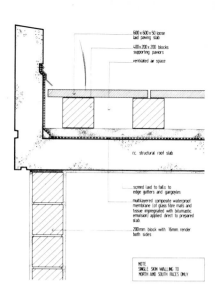

Architectural fabric was used in Brunei for the State Reception tented structure, of catenary tensile design, as further described in the adjoining caption.

Two instances of innovatory specification of roofing materials are first, the realisation, as early as any other overseas architects, that positioning thermal insulation on top of the roof structure – 'upside-down construction' as it has become known – was the way, under many circumstances, to make full use of thermal insulation, as illustrated above; and second, an early use in the Gulf of the 'Hypalon' single-ply roofing membrane that made possible the continuous horizontal and sloping planes of Al Itehad School roof.

Top   two alternative detail design cross-section drawing for 'upside-down' (inverted) roof construction, whereby the waterproofing layer, which is laid directly on top of the structural roof, is protected by the thermal insulation from exposure to sunlight. The firm was one of the first to adopt this method, before it became publicised and generally accepted.

Above   Low-cost Bachelor Flats, Oman; coursed, rendered blockwork and perforated concrete block screen wall and roof balconies.

Ceremonial Marquee for H.M. The Sultan of Brunei; the tensile structure 85.5m × 27.5m × 15m high for the accommodation of 3,000 guests, was fabricated in the U.K. and despatched complete by air with a rigging team for erection on site. Design and manufacture was completed in six weeks. The tent covers an area of 2,915m² and the covering membrane is a flameproofed polyester fabric coated with orange coloured PVC.

Solar control

Control of solar heat gain and sunlight glare are not only the related, main architectural determinants in southerly countries, but they are also of increasing significance in European contexts at a time when 'low-energy' building design becomes ever more important. When John Harris first worked overseas, refrigerant air-conditioning was only just being introduced, and reflective heat-absorbing solar glass did not exist. Accordingly, 'natural' architectural methods of improving conditions within buildings had to be adopted. Subsequently, where both have become available, they are used as economically as possible in *secondary* roles, to back up natural elevational shading and ventilation provisions. In many developing Third World countries, however, neither air-conditioning nor solar glass is likely to be other than exceptionally possible, and architectural methods must retain their relevance as the only means of providing enhanced interior comfort conditions.

As evolved from the early John R Harris designs for the Kuwait Building Research Establishment Laboratories, and the State (Rumaillah) Hospital at Doha, need for solar control has determined the planning and elevational appearance of the firm's overseas work in three main ways:

first, the orientation of buildings on an east-west axis, with minimal, end-wall elevational exposure to the *low* sun angles of morning, and especially late afternoon and evening. High sun angles of midday, on

The Trade Centre Tower, Dubai; looking up the perimeter sun-shade screen, with its subtly evocative arch-form derived from local Islamic tradition.

Left The British Ambassador's Residence, Abu Dhabi; the 'porte-cochere' timber shade structure.
Above an existing house in Muscat, Oman, for which the local office of John R Harris Associates designed timber sun-shading screens.

southern elevations, ordinarily present no great problems that cannot be solved by simple projections;

second, where site constraints make that ideal orientation difficult or impossible, various planning devices have been developed by the firm to enable vulnerable room windows to be correctly orientated;

third, elevational sun-shading whereby projecting vertical and

The Dubai Hospital; looking up the tower, showing the serrated floor plan, which provides shading for perimeter windows, and also the use of a proprietary metal sun-shading grille system.

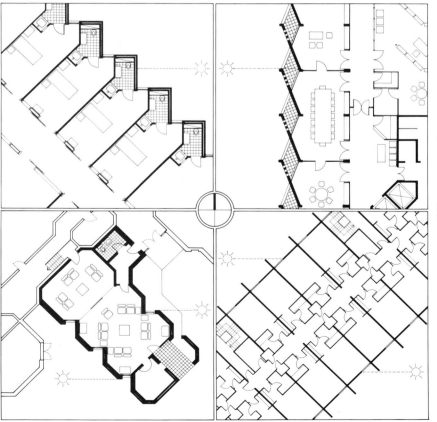

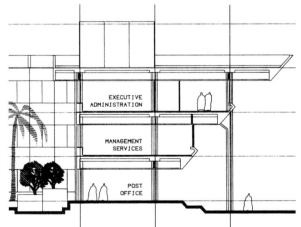

Simple eaves roof overhang for elevational sun-shading at Al Maktoum Hospital, one of the firm's early buildings in the Gulf.

CAAD facility cross-section drawing of an administrative building in the Arabian Gulf, showing the projecting upper floors, providing shade for those below.

Four diagrammatic architectural planning methods, taken from the firm's practice, of providing sun-shading for windows on elevations that are unavoidably orientated other than north-south (north at the top in all cases).

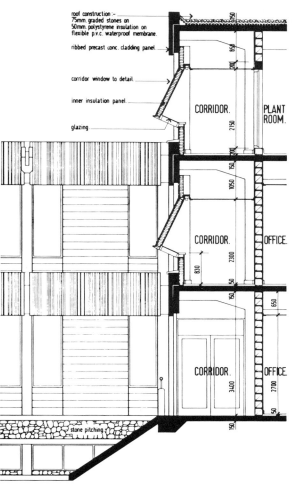

roof construction :—
75mm. graded stones on
50mm. polystyrene insulation on
flexible p.v.c. waterproof membrane.

ribbed precast conc. cladding panel

corridor window to detail

inner insulation panel

glazing

CORRIDOR. | PLANT ROOM.

CORRIDOR. | OFFICE.

CORRIDOR. | OFFICE.

stone pitching

Government office building, Oman; the section and detail elevational view, of shaded downward-angled windows on an east-west facing circulation spine.

horizontal parts of the structure, or comparable non-structural components – such as louvres and grilles – prevent direct sunlight entering important interior spaces.

The buildings illustrated on these four pages show a variety of responses to the need for solar control. The Trade Centre tower in Dubai posed the particularly demanding problem of a square-shaped floor plan with equally important office windows on all four sides. After calculation and setting out of sun-angles involved, the ideal orientation was found to be diagonally to the cardinal points within an enveloping precast concrete screen.

The Dubai Hospital exemplifies elevational modelling to convert to north/south ward window exposure, in combination with a lightweight proprietory solar grille system; and four planning examples are shown diagrammatically on the facing page. An unusual, innovatory detail design response to unavoidable east/west exposure of part of a government building complex in Oman, took the form of downward angled windows admitting controlled, reflected light (section and view, above).

Historical associations

A strong sense of history is evident in the firm's work, both in the design of new buildings for specific historic locations and cultural contexts, and also in the restoration of old buildings. The buildings and designs illustrated on these four pages exemplify these aspects of the work, with reference to others elsewhere in the book.

Where there is an established historic location for a new building, such as the High Street, Winchester, England, shown opposite, a first architectural consideration is the creation of a 'well-mannered neighbour', which will fit in with the existing urban character, at the same time as establishing its own identity. Compatibility of scale and massing, choice of sympathetic facing materials, and appropriate detail elevational designing are pre-requisites in this respect. Elsewhere in the UK, Thorney Court Apartments, and Park Hospital, are further examples of this concern for place, respectively those of central London, facing Kensington Gardens, and rural Nottinghamshire, alongside a country park.

96, 47

Abroad, although most new buildings have been designed for newly developed urban districts, even 'new towns', without immediate historic characters, there are important exceptions, one of the most pleasing of which is the new Grindlay's Bank (originally the Ottoman Bank) just outside the old city wall of Muscat, the historic capital of the Sultanate of Oman.

This is an architecture which is unmistakably both of its time and place; an achievement deriving not only from use of local materials – in this case, rendered concrete blockwork and timber screening; but also, and more so, a respect for indigenous cultural traditions. The small proportion of openings to solid wall are the traditional response to climate, as also the projecting balcony to shade the ground floor windows, and there is also a 'fortress' reference appropriate alike to its function as one of the first banks in the Sultanate, and the defen-

Grindlay's Bank Building, Muscat, Oman; the new building, designed originally for the Ottoman Bank, seen against the mountainous backcloth, with its historic neighbours, just outside the old city wall.

WINCHESTER PROJE
JOHN R. HARRIS Architects

Top design sketches for housing in Brunei derived from study of traditional vernacular forms.
Centre design model for a commercial development in the High Street, Winchester, England, illustrating a concern to create a new street architecture in keeping with the historic context.
Below a Heliport in Brunei, designed in sympathy with local traditional architecture, while fulfilling the stringent functional requirements of a modern building type.

sive nature of local historic architecture. The National Bank of Dubai
71 building at Abra Point, alongside the Creek in Dubai, is another
highly successful integration of a modern building into an historic
context.

Generally, abroad, identification with local cultural traditions con-
stitutes a point of departure for new building designs, as further
illustrated by the conceptual sketches for housing in Brunei; and the
23 Heliport for the Government of Brunei.

The second broad area of historical association is an involvement
with the special requirements of historic national building restoration. In London, the most significant work of this kind has been at
the Natural History Museum where the magnificent interior of the

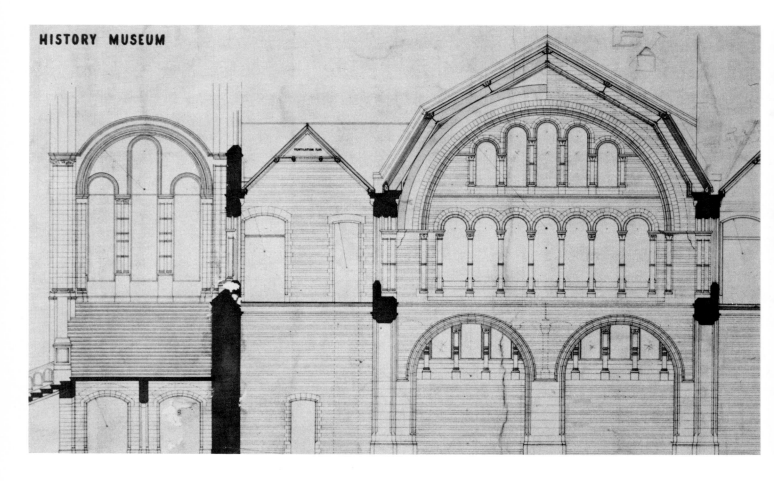

North Hall designed by Alfred Waterhouse and completed in 1881,
37 has been fully restored to its original Victorian splendour. This work
involved the cleaning and retouching of the hand-painted plaster
ceiling panels; general interior refurbishing and cleaning the terra
cotta wall tiling; and the installation of a new low-level lighting
system. Externally, the roof was repaired and fully reslated. The
work also includes the Main Hall and the East Galleries.

Abroad, as an example of this work, the British Council in Muscat
was persuaded that a restored and appropriately modernised historic
building in Mutrah would make a more suitable centre for its extended activities in Oman, than a part of an anonymous modern office
building. John R Harris Associates found a suitable old, near-derelict
building, dating from the 1870s, arranged the lease, and carried
through a sensitively conceived restoration and refitting building
programme.

The Natural History Museum, South Kensington,
London; the original cross-section drawing by Alfred
Waterhouse through the entrance hall, and the North
Hall on the right. The restored ceiling with its beautiful
paintings is illustrated in colour on page 37.

The British Council Building, Mutrah, Oman; two views
of the old Omani building which was restored and refitted
as the Council's headquarters. The view above shows
the beautiful Mutrah Bay, with the fort to the right, seen
from the first floor terrace; the view below is of the
terrace with timber screening designed by the firm in the
local tradition.

Landscape: contexts and planning

The broad international spread of work has involved designing in terms of a great variety of landscape contexts. As examples, these range from the site for Park Hospital adjoining wooded parkland in the English countryside, where a primary concern was to create an architecture in keeping with the natural beauty; to the arid desert location of Haima Tribal Centre, in Oman, not far distant from the aptly named 'Empty Quarter' of the Arabian peninsular, where a completely new human place had to be created.

Ordinarily, the landscaping of surrounds and interiors of buildings is designed within the firm, but on occasion, as required by clients, there has been the involvement of a landscape architect as a specialist consultant. One such instance illustrated is the Stoke Mandeville Hospital courtyards and exterior landscaping.

Stoke Mandeville Hospital, Aylesbury; the view of a landscaped courtyard from an out-patient waiting area.

The pools, fountains and cascades at the International Trade Centre, Dubai, the Hilton Hotel in the background.

Water has always played a major part in the creation of pleasant settings and interiors for buildings, notable examples of which are the pools, fountains and cascades at the Trade Centre, and also those at the entrance to Rashid Hospital, both in Dubai.

In addition to the design of landscape settings for their buildings, the firm has also been involved in urban landscaping proposals of a general nature. Two examples are illustrated: first, the design for the major traffic roundabout adjoining the Trade Centre in Dubai which

The pool and fountains in front of the main entrance of Rashid Hospital; the 'white-water' effect of the fountains is created by mixing air with the recirculated water.

Templemead, a private house planned on one floor in the orchard garden of an Edwardian house.

The landscape character of the site influenced the plan and character of the new building, and vistas from the large house were respected.

30

Park Hospital, Nottinghamshire, England; the buildings of this private hospital were designed to fit unobtrusively into the adjoining mature wooded landscape of Sherwood Forest.

as a computer plot is notable for acceptance by the Royal Academy for the 1983 Summer Exhibition in London; and second, the Deira Creek Study, Dubai, which included a new waterfront civic square in front of the Municipality Building. Both were competition winning designs. The Urban Development Plan proposals for the Zhuhai Special Economic Zone of the People's Republic of China, include the landscaping of a leisure and recreation resort area centred on an 18-hole golf course and a public park and yacht marina.

The swimming pool and courtyard planting at Chenestone, a private house on the south coast of England.

29

The firm's winning entry in the international urban landscaping competition for the Deira creekside, Dubai.

Far left   a part computer plot produced by the firm's CAAD facility, of urban landscaping proposals for the large traffic roundabout adjoining the Dubai International Trade Centre. The design is based on a free-form layout of linked octagonal elements comprising fountains, water features, shaded rest areas, and hard and soft landscaping. A pedestrian bridge connects the Roundabout to the Trade Centre site. The colour computer plot was accepted for the 1983 Summer Exhibition of the Royal Academy, London.

Above   a detail view of residential landscaping for the Government in Oman.

Left   luxuriant shaded planting in the garden of a new majlis, designed by the firm, adjoining an existing house in Muscat, Oman.

Ones that got away

From the initial competition success of 1953 for the new State Hospital at Doha, Qatar, through to the present day, there has been a consistent commitment to the several forms of architectural competition that have evolved over the years. Primarily, of course, this has been with the intention of winning and receiving the commission to build the design. John Harris himself believes that, on entering a competition, no endeavour must be spared until the final day arrives for the submission. Competitions are won by those architects who think deeply about them.

But even though the firm can be confidently said to have won more competitions of various kinds than other British architects during the period, realism cautions: 'you cannot win them all'. Accordingly, the preparation of a competition entry has a secondary purpose whereby new ideas can be investigated and a stimulus provided for the design teams involved.

These four pages illustrate a number of competition designs that 'got away'; or which were successful in gaining the commission only to require subsequent revision out of recognition. Of the former category, the designs for the High Court Building, Brunei; and the Abbey National Society's new Headquarters Building, Milton Keynes, are favourites of the architects concerned. The Ministry of Social Affairs and Labour, Muscat, Oman, exemplifies a winner that was greatly changed when built by the firm.

Top right one of the competition-winning elevational drawings for the Ministry of Social Affairs and Labour Headquarters Building, at Al Khuweir Diplomatic City, Oman; the design was subsequently changed in response to revised government requirements, to that illustrated on page 81.
Centre right cross-section drawing of a Diwan in Abu Dhabi.
Bottom right the design for a new computer centre in Central Milton Keynes, England. The client's brief was for 20,000m² of accommodation, as a phased development programme.
Below the High Court Building designed for a riverside site in Bandar Seri Begawan, the capital of Brunei.

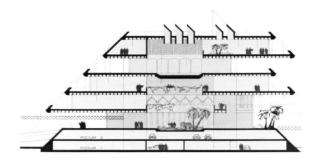

Above the competition entry for the Municipality Building, Dubai.
Below The International Trade Centre, Dubai; a lowrise scheme, replaced by the skyscraper design as constructed.

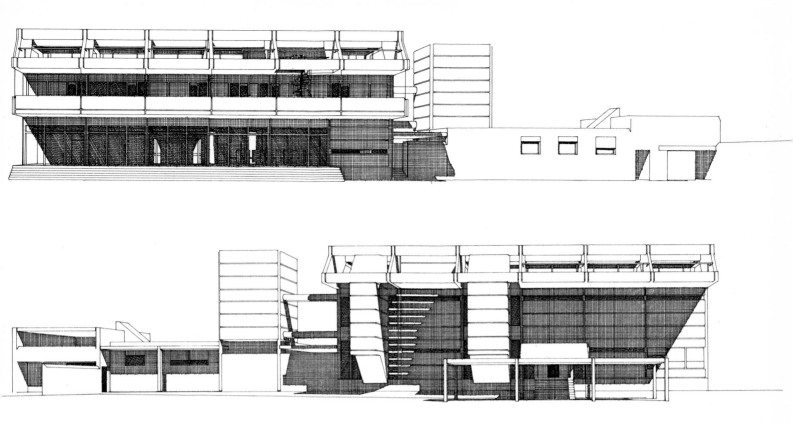

In addition, there are early designs for projects that were replaced by an alternative during the planning stages. The first design for the Dubai Trade Centre had a pronounced horizontal emphasis which was converted, at the client's request, into the vertical form of the Arabian Gulf's first true skyscraper. Other designs commissioned through normal client/architect relationships have eventually had to be abandoned, or replaced, for various reasons, to exist only in model form, or on paper – as beautifully illustrated by the elevational perspectives for the proposed British Ambassador's Residence at Baghdad.

Top elevational perspective sketches of the proposed British Ambassador's Residence, Baghdad, Iraq.
Above an early proposal for the National Bank of Dubai Building, Dubai.
Left the competition entry for the design of a new Oriental Museum at the University of Durham, England.

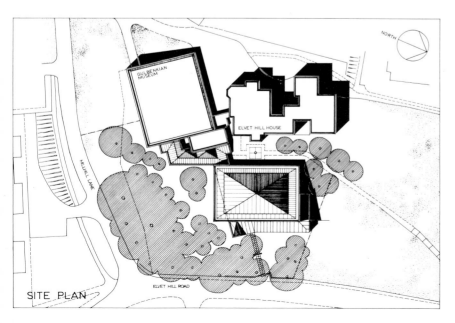

SITE PLAN

Refurbishment

There has been varied work in the fields of refurbishment and conversion of existing buildings. In addition to the European examples shown on these two pages, there have also been comparable involvements abroad, notably for the British Council at Mutrah, in the Sultanate of Oman.

Two contracts for the refurbishment of residential buildings were carried out for the Property Services Agency in London for the rehabilitation and improvement of married families quarters for ceremonial troops based in the capital. These are Jubilee Buildings at St John's Wood Barracks, for the King's Troop of the Royal Horse Artillery; and Queen Mary's Buildings in Victoria.

Two further commissions have involved work within important historic buildings in London and Paris; first, the Headquarters for the London Brick PLC, in a Nash terrace adjoining Regent's Park; and second, the Paris offices of the Legal and General Assurance Society in Rue de la Victoire.

There was also an unusual educational building requirement whereby a new assembly hall for Wellesley House Preparatory School, Broadstairs, Kent, incorporated the old chapel, with its organ, of nearby St Peter's Court School, when the two establishments were merged.

The London Brick PLC offices, London; restoration and conversion of an historic Regent's Park terrace.

Below   Queen Mary's Buildings, Victoria; and
Left   Jubilee Buildings, St John's Wood; the rehabilitation and improvement of married quarters for the Royal Horse Artillery and ceremonial troops in London.

Natural History Museum, London; the ceiling of the
North Hall restored as part of the restoration programme
carried out by the firm.

25 Rue de la Victoire, Paris; refurbishment and conversion as offices for the Legal and General Assurance
Society.

The well-ordered plan

The continuing characteristic of the architectural planning over the years is an emphasis on clearly defined relationships between the parts of complex functional programmes. An ability to produce order out of the often conflicting requirements on a major hospital brief, has been a pre-requisite of the international health buildings field – in particular when designing in competition with others – and the disciplines involved have clearly influenced their work in general.

The organisation of the departments and other activities comprising the podium levels of the Dubai Hospital illustrates this concern for the 'well-ordered plan'. The proposal for a Phased Development Hospital, Dubai, resulted in an ingenious ultimate square plan (half of which is shown below) with 45° diagonal axes at the corners. The plan of the Mental Hospital at Jumeira, Dubai, also derives from a 45° diagonal response to the need for north/south orientation of the main rooms.

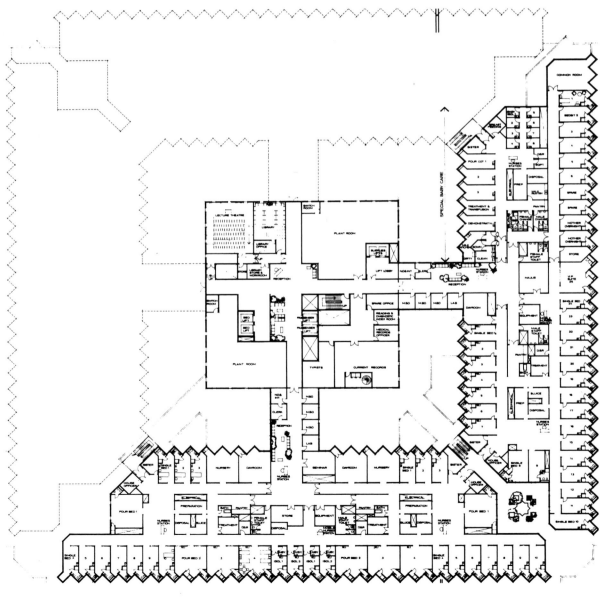

The Phased Development Hospital, Dubai; the plan at an intermediate growth stage, comprising two sides of a square, and the central block. The subsequent addition of one or both of the remaining two sides would be facilitated by the 45° splay of the ends of the completed sides.

Planning is generally on an orthogonal grid basis; an approach that has tended to be consolidated in response to the extra-special design requirements involved in working with a computer aided architectural design (CAAD) facility. Examples illustrated include a part ward floor plan of Tuen Mun Hospital, Hong Kong. But building plans are also tailored to meet individual site requirements, both in terms of an existing building context – as exemplified by the non-rectangular shaping of Thorney Court in London; and also as determined by climatic considerations, notably the use of hexagons, with shaded corner windows, for the DOHMS Headquarters Building in Dubai. Need for shaded exterior teaching and leisure spaces, usable at various times of day, determined the economically orthogonal layout of Al Itehad School, also in Dubai, with its articulated arrangement of separate linked pavilions.

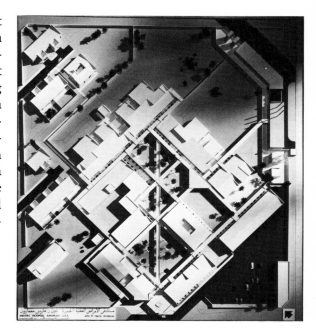

The Mental Hospital, Jumeira; the east-west orientation of the buildings has placed them at an angle of 45° to the site boundaries, and a main circulation route through the hospital is therefore planned as a diagonal axis.

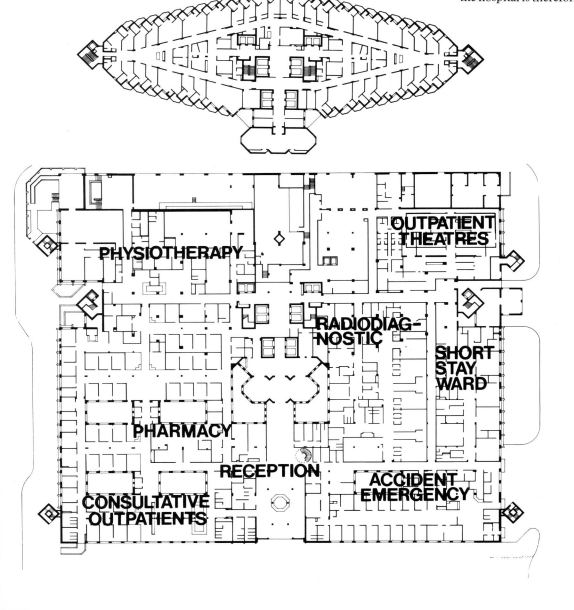

PHYSIOTHERAPY

OUTPATIENT THEATRES

RADIODIAG-NOSTIC

SHORT STAY WARD

PHARMACY

RECEPTION

ACCIDENT EMERGENCY

CONSULTATIVE OUTPATIENTS

The ground level podium plan and the typical tower floor plan of the Dubai Hospital, exemplifying the 'well-ordered' planning.

Interiors

These three pages illustrate a number of important examples of the interior design work of the firm in the UK and abroad. The range is very extensive, encompassing the contrasted scales, and requirements of English domestic interiors and grand international hotels; office skyscraper entrance lobbies and hospital wards; and the economic possibilities of luxury London apartments and the simplest overseas housing accommodation.

The interiors of all buildings are ordinarily designed within the firm, by the architects concerned, making use of specialist interior decoration, lighting and furnishing advice where required by the nature of the work. A strong preference for the use of natural materials is a characteristic, exemplified here by the timber boarded ceiling of the House at Swain's Wood, and the polished travertine of walls in the Dubai Hilton Hotel's public rooms. The Al Itehad School, Dubai,

Right   doors at the Hilton Hotel, Dubai, designed in the local tradition for palace and similar prestigious doors.
Below right   a swimming pool constructed in the basement of a luxury residence in Mayfair, London.

Left   the sitting room of Swains Wood, illustrating the use of natural materials for ceiling and walls; and the relationship with the landscape extending across the Chilterns to Henley.
Below left   looking up a stairwell, Brunei Shell Recreation Club, Seria, Negara Brunei Darussalam.
Below   the interior design for a residence conversion, Hyde Park, London.

The Penthouse Apartment, National Bank of Dubai; designed for the general manager of the Bank, to provide special facilities for banquets and receptions. The view is of the landscaped, air-conditioned internal courtyard.

makes excellent, economic use of timber-faced construction components in this respect.

Great care is taken to relate decorative motifs and design details to those of a local cultural tradition. In Oman, the screens in a Government club are designed in this way, and the grand wooden and brass doors in the Dubai Hilton are an extremely successful modern interpretation of traditional craft. Elsewhere in the book, the conversion of an old building in Mutrah, Oman, for the British Council; the architect's own offices in London; and the interiors of the Royal Brunei 116 Polo Club pavilion, are further examples of locally relevant interiors.

Decorative doors and screens for a government club, Oman; the design is based on local traditional patterns.

PART TWO

The second part of the book illustrates a wide range of the work of The John R. Harris Group, arranged in broad building type categories. Each building type has its own summary introduction.

Health

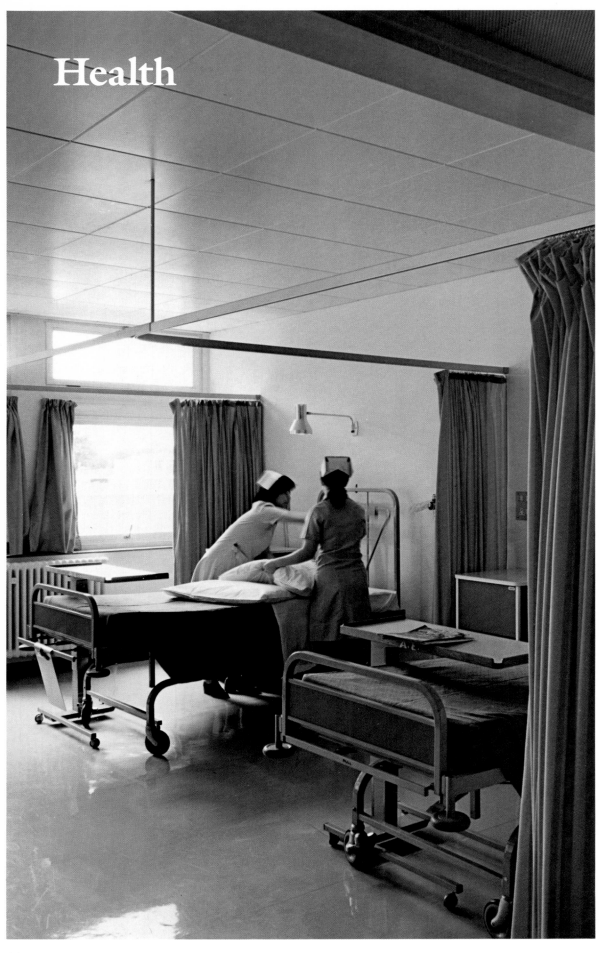

A typical four-bed ward at Ealing District Hospital.

Ealing District Hospital
The 3-storey podium contains casualty, theatres, X-ray, outpatient, general treatment and administrative departments. The podium adjoins a seven-storey ward block providing 406 beds for general and specialist use.

Health

In addition to the building of new hospitals as such in a total of 12 countries, The John R. Harris Group has also been responsible for a wide range of related new health service developments, including: administrative offices and computer centres, medical supplies and laundry facilities, kitchens, laboratories, dental centres and clinics for a variety of specialist requirements. As a more recent aspect of this work, the firm has been responsible for several new private hospitals in the United Kingdom. There has also been international involvement in numerous major renovation improvement and extension programmes for existing hospitals and health service buildings.

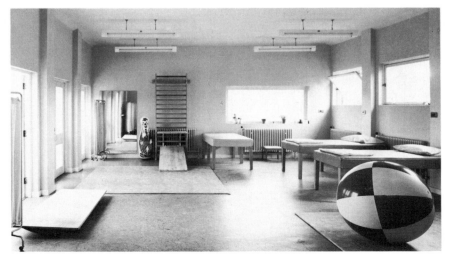

Top **King Edward VII Hospital, Windsor**
The new Outpatients and Accident Department, which forms part of the redevelopment of the hospital to become a full District Hospital.

Centre **Stoke Mandeville Hospital, Buckinghamshire**
Five phases of development are proposed to provide an eventual total of 1,500 beds. The initial phase of 350 beds includes Outpatient, Orthopaedic and Fracture, Accident and Emergency, Intensive Therapy and Operating Departments.

Left **Harperbury Hospital, Harperbury**
A Cerebral Palsy unit designed for research, and training of staff in the specialist treatment and rehabilitation of spastic children. The Centre was provided by, and designed in association with the Nuffield Trust.

Park Hospital, Nottinghamshire
Park Hospital is a private health care venture planned as two separate but linked blocks, one of which provides 50 private rooms on two storeys, and the other, on one storey, contains a 3-theatre suite with ITU, pathology, pharmacy, physiotherapy and X-ray departments. In addition there are consulting suites, administrative offices, staff dining room and kitchens. The building is of brick, with pantile roofs, situated within the Country Park which is part of the ancient Sherwood Forest.

Ealing District Hospital/
Queen Charlotte's Hospital
The overall site development model, which was exhibited at the Summer Exhibition of the Royal Academy, relating the Ealing District Hospital to the left, with the proposed new buildings for Queen Charlotte's Hospital for Women.

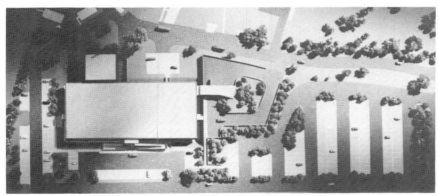

Dispensary and Dental Clinic, Bentwaters, Suffolk

A two-storey building which provides medical facilities for base personnel and their families. The large dental clinic occupies the ground floor, and the first floor provides accommodation for offices, pharmacy, radiology, pathology, examination and consultation suites, and accident and emergency departments. The building is fully air-conditioned for comfort and to assist sound insulation from the high level of aircraft noise.

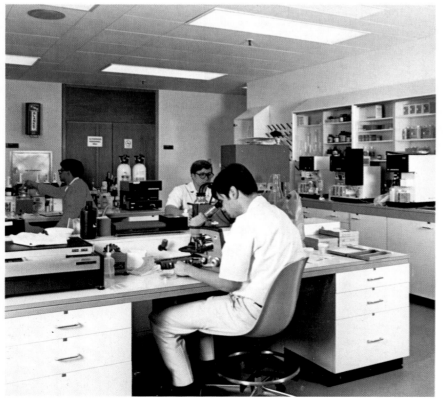

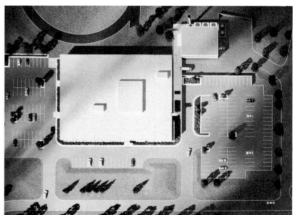

Composite Medical Facility, Upper Heyford, Oxfordshire

This hospital provides inpatient and outpatient facilities for base personnel and their families. There are 60 inpatient beds for medical, surgical, intensive care, obstetric and paediatric patients; a surgical suite, and delivery and nursery suites. Outpatient facilities include clinics and dental treatment suites; radiology, pharmacy and pathology support, and a physical medical department. The building was designed to be constructed using an industrialised building system and special measures were adopted, after research, to ensure adequate insulation against high levels of aircraft noise.

49

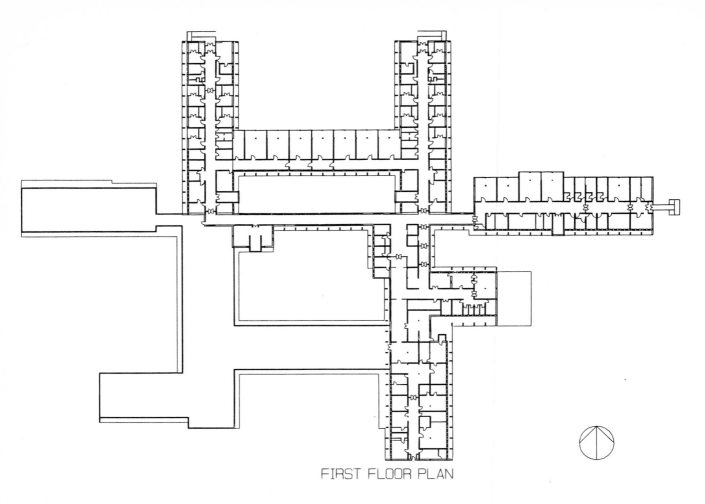

FIRST FLOOR PLAN

Rumaillah Hospital, Doha, Qatar
The ground and first floor plans of the hospital which was opened, originally, as the State Hospital in 1957. The two plans have been drawn by the firm's CAAD facility as the basis of the refurbishment of the hospital as a post-operative recuperation and geriatric hospital.

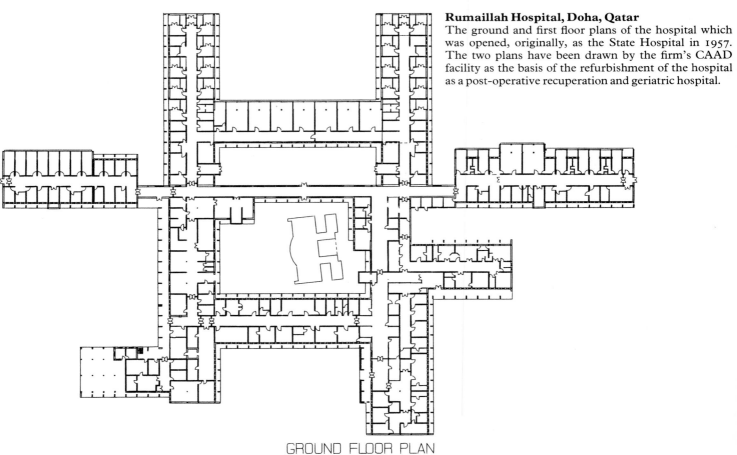

GROUND FLOOR PLAN

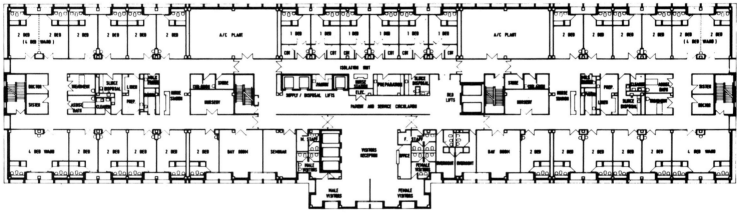

The New Women's Hospital, Doha, Qatar

The new specialist hospital of 322 beds on five ward floors, will be operated independently, but with some shared services with the adjoining new general hospital. It replaces the original single storey women's hospital in Doha which was completed by the firm in 1958, and which has been run in conjunction with Rumaillah Hospital.

The perspective drawing shows the New Women's Hospital from the south-west, with the recessed shaded windows of the long southern elevation; the floor plan is typical, with minor variations.

Below the mid-1950's layout of the single storey original Women's Hospital.

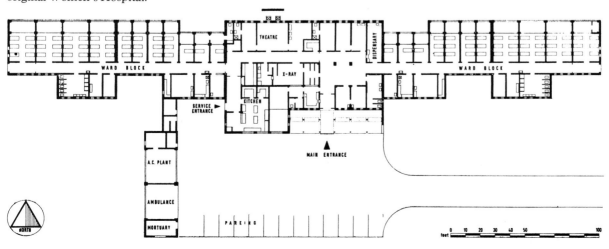

The Dubai Hospital

The hospital is located on the Deira side of the Creek which divides the city of Dubai into two parts. John R Harris and Partners were appointed architects for the project following an open international competition in which their scheme was awarded the first premium. The hospital provides a total of 665 beds planned on the ten floors of the tower which rises above a two-storey podium containing the administrative, surgical and medical departments.

Top left   a view of the hospital showing the relationship of the tower and the podium;
Bottom left   the shaded entrance and waiting area;
Left   the main entrance hall;
Below   the hospital as seen across the Deira rooftops.

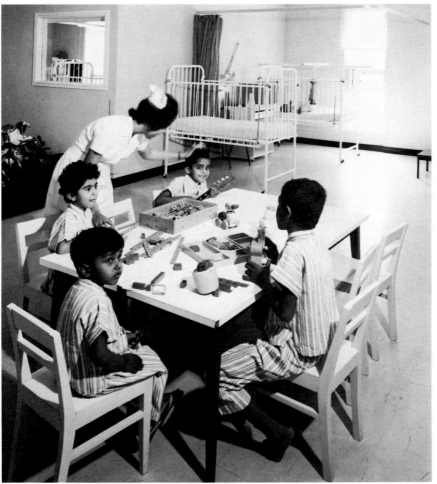

The Rashid Hospital, Dubai

A general hospital for the city of Dubai and the surrounding region, which was designed and constructed in three years, on the instructions of His Highness Sheikh Rashid, Ruler of Dubai. 400 beds were provided by the first phase construction and a second phase added a further 230 beds.

Top   a general view of the hospital (see also page 28 for photograph of the entrance domes);
Above   the main hospital kitchens;
Left   the Children's Ward.

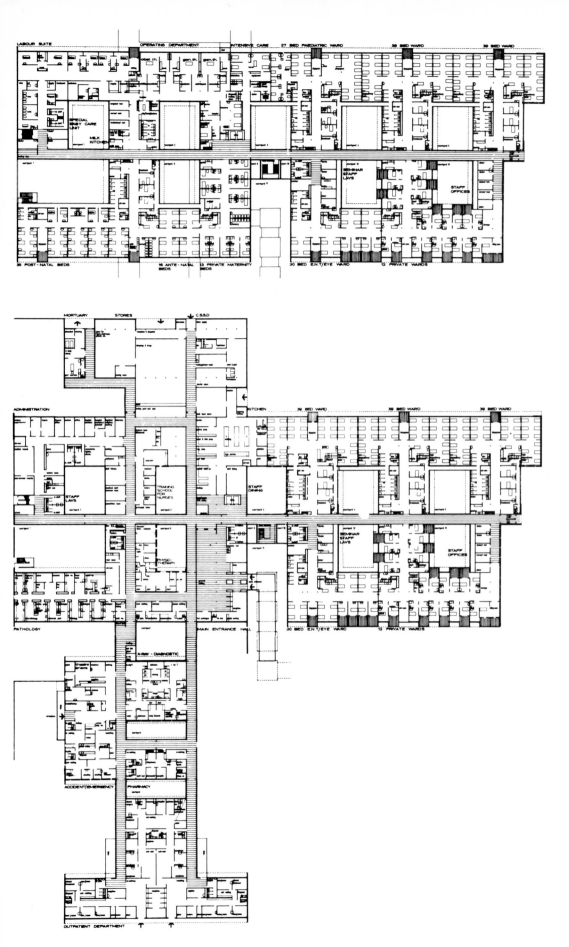

Ground and first floor plans of The Rashid Hospital,
Dubai.

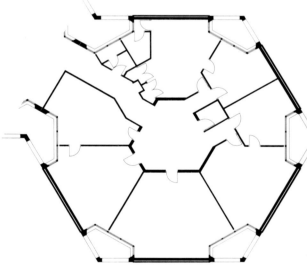

Headquarters Building, The Department of Health and Medical Services, Dubai

The building houses management, finance, planning, secretarial and office staff for the entire Dubai Health Service. There is a Presidential suite and offices for the Director and his management staff. The building complex also incorporates a major computer suite.

The part plan is of one of the hexagonal wings of the building, with recessed corner windows for sunshading.

**The Medical Services Development Plan,
Abu Dhabi**
The plan proposals included an acute general hospital
with 391 beds for the City of Abu Dhabi, as illustrated.

**The Central Medical Services Supply Building,
Dubai**

Sulaibikhat Hospital, Kuwait

The hospital provides comprehensive inpatient and out-patient facilities for the specialist treatment of women. The wards, containing 406 general beds, enjoy the cooler northern aspect and have views out across the Arabian Gulf. A Premature Baby Unit of 97 beds has been added as a second phase of the overall longterm development of the hospital.

One of the three 4-storey ward blocks, showing the narrow vertical windows recessed between panels of facing brickwork for sun-shading. The sand-lime bricks were produced in a local plant which John R Harris helped to develop.

Two detail elevational views of Sulaibikhat Hospital

Tuen Mun Hospital, Hong Kong

The design of this 1,606 bed district general hospital for the Hong Kong government is based on the need to separate the 1,266 acute and general beds from the 340 beds for psychiatric and mentally retarded patients. This is achieved by placing the general wards and operating theatres in an 11-storey double-cruciform block, above a podium containing services; with the psychiatric and mentally retarded wards located in a separate 4-storey block. The two parts are linked by the main entrance atrium, which also houses the staff canteens and medical library. There are also separate blocks for Pathology and Radiotherapy departments.

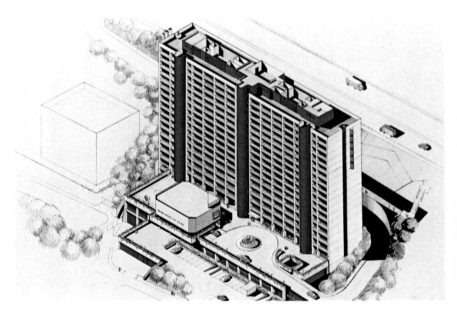

Caritas Medical Centre, Hong Kong

The Medical Centre, which was established in 1964, is situated to serve the densely populated areas of So Uk, Cheung Sha Wan, Shek Kip Mei, and Sham Shui Po. The new extension will provide accommodation on seven lower floors for facilities which will support and serve the entire multi-building hospital complex. These facilities include: Pharmacy, Central Sterile Supply Department, a new Training School, Administrative Offices, and kitchens. The upper twelve floors will provide flats for various grades of medical staff, 182 rooms for nurses, and training and leisure areas.

60

The University of Maiduguri Teaching Hospital, Maiduguri, Nigeria

The new hospital is located in north-eastern Nigeria serving a large population. Accommodation provided includes 600 in-patient beds, with fully equipped operating theatre suites, and other specialist departments, including Obstetric and Radiodiagnostic departments. The hospital is generally of two-storey construction, as shown by the aerial photograph on page 14, with a 4-storey block identifying the main entrance, as above.

Below left **Kiulap General Hospital, Negara Brunei Darussalam;** for which John R Harris was the Technical Architectural Adviser.

Below right **Kuala Lumpur State Hospital, Malaysia;** for which John R Harris was the Consultant Architect.

Al Nahda Hospital, Muscat, Oman
This was the first major hospital development completed
in the Sultanate of Oman. It forms part of the initial
Regional Development Plan, drawn up by John R Harris,
and the programme for health services development.

Hospital Development, Oman

Fujairah Hospital, UAE

Sharjah Hospital, UAE

Phased Development Hospital, Dubai, UAE

Commercial

The Dubai International Trade Centre, from the east.

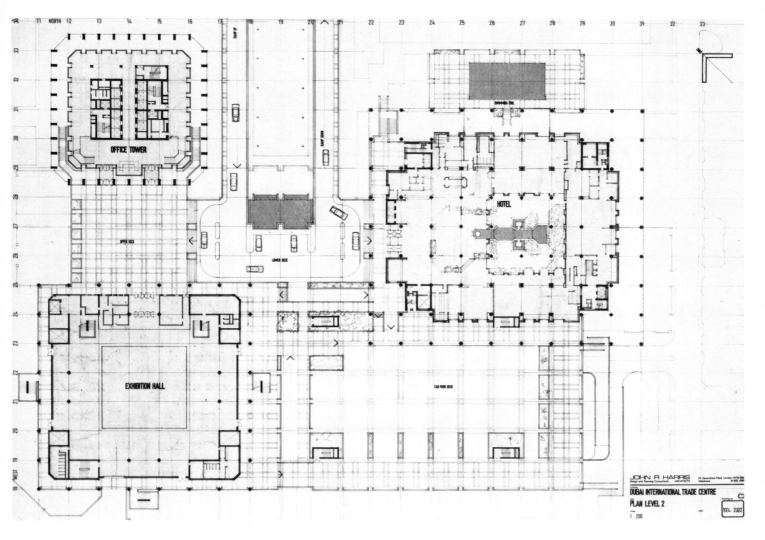

JOHN R HARRIS
Design and Planning Consultants   ARCHITECTS
DUBAI INTERNATIONAL TRADE CENTRE
PLAN LEVEL 2
1:200

Commercial

The work of The John R. Harris Group in this broad field extends in
scale from individual buildings – such as Banks and a wide range of
commercial developments; through to the design and grouping of a
number of buildings to form a major commercial development, such
as the International Trade Centre at Dubai, with its 39-storey office
tower, conference and exhibition centre, multi-storey appartments,
and the Dubai Hilton Hotel. In addition, there has been a continuing
programme of major city centre commercial developments in the
United Kingdom and Europe.

The Dubai International Trade Centre
The plan at the raised entrance level of the main floor of
the Trade Centre; the approach and exit ramps, from
ground level, are adjoining the tower at the northern
corner of the site. The 39-storey office tower is
orientated diagonally north-south for optimum solar
control purposes; the typical office floor is shown below.

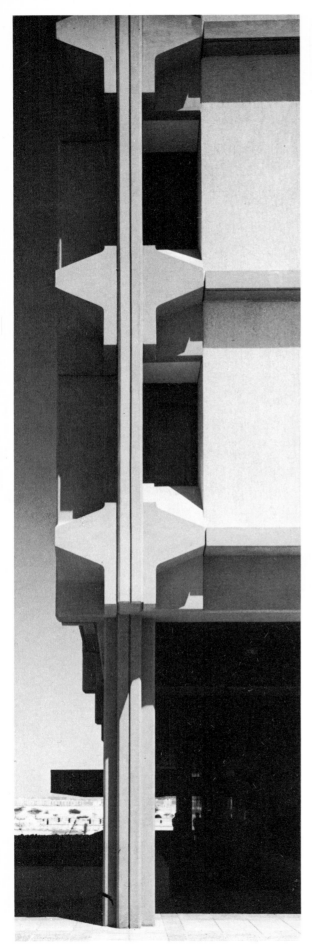

The Dubai International Trade Centre
Left a close-up of the concrete detailing at the corner of the Dubai Hilton Hotel, showing the recessed, shaded bedroom windows;
Above left the multi-purpose Exhibition Hall in the foreground, with the office tower beyond;
Right an interior view of the Hall with a trade exhibition in progress.

The central courtyard of the Dubai Hilton Hotel showing the fountains and pools which are linked by a cascade to the pool in the lobby.

International Hotel Development, South China Sea.

The Dubai Metropolitan Hotel, Dubai
The hotel is situated on the main Dubai – Abu Dhabi
highway, a short distance from the Dubai International
Trade Centre.

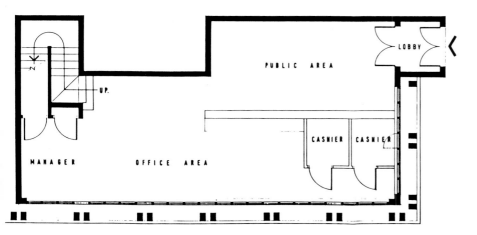

**The National Bank of Dubai
Abra Point Branch, Dubai**
The new two-storey branch bank is located on the Creek
edge. The banking hall, and offices at first floor level,
enjoy impressive views across the shipping movements
to the far side of the Creek. The location required the use
of special piled foundations.
Left   looking past the Bank entrance towards the Creek
and the Abra landing stage;
Above   the reverse view of the Bank's waterside location; and the plans at ground and first floor levels.

ROOF TERRACE

DOWN

LOBBY

OFFICE AREA

FEM.
LAV.

MALE
LAV.

KITCHEN

FIRST FLOOR

UP.

LOBBY

PUBLIC AREA

CASHIER   CASHIER

MANAGER   OFFICE AREA

The National Bank of Dubai, Dubai

The Bank Headquarters Building occupies a waterfront site overlooking Dubai Creek and harbour. The main banking hall and ancillary accommodation is at ground and mezzanine levels; above are four floors of administrative offices, with a penthouse apartment over.

The two photographs show the Creek as seen from the building, and the Creek elevation at night.

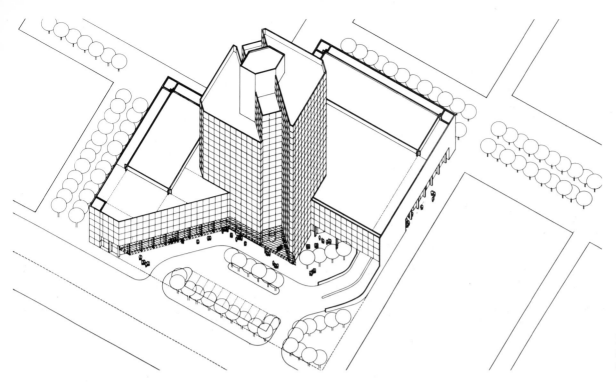

Haba Office Building and Commercial Centre, Qatar

The British Bank of the Middle East, Salalah, Oman.

Risail Commercial Centre, Capital Area, Oman
A group of fifteen shops, a large supermarket and a restaurant, near the International Airport, on the main highway from Seeb to Muscat.

Three city centre redevelopments in Europe;
top, above, below Antwerp;
left Strasbourg;
below left Brussels.

Two shopping centre developments in the United Kingdom; *top* Cwmbran, seen beyond attractive town centre landscaping; *left* west London.

WESTMINSTER BANK

Westminster Bank, Gunnersbury, London
Top and above   two views of the exterior and interior
of the branch bank building in West London.

**John R Harris Architects, the firm's offices
24 Devonshire Place, London W1**
Right   plans of the existing Devonshire Place house,
and the new split-level offices at the rear, entered from
Marylebone High Street. The photograph shows the
courtyard with the linking gallery to the right.

**Office Building Development, Marylebone Road,
London**

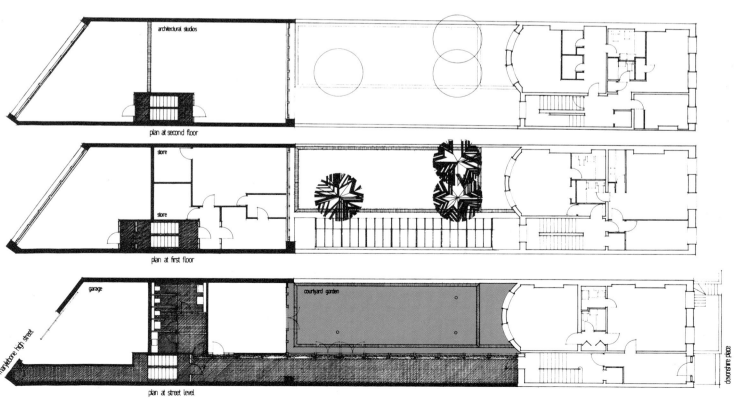

architectural studios

plan at second floor

store

store

plan at first floor

garage

courtyard garden

plan at street level

marylebone high street

devonshire place

Governmental

Administrative offices, Muscat, Oman
The building was designed as the first phase of government building development in the historic walled city of Muscat.

Governmental

This building type comprises examples of work for government agencies as the client. In addition to government buildings as such, there are also administrative offices and residential buildings included under this heading.

Left Waterside buildings of a naval base development in the Sultanate of Oman.

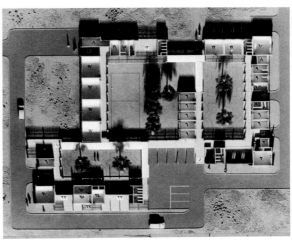

Haima Tribal Centre, Oman

The tribal centre provides administrative and social welfare facilities for some 10,000 nomadic tribesmen in the isolated interior Jiddat Al-Hirasis region of Oman. The main facilities are grouped around three courtyards and include a four-classroom school, a health clinic, administrative offices for the local Wali – the local ruler responsible to the Ministry of the Interior – and a supermarket. Nearby, there is also a mosque, residential accommodation, a children's hostel and canteen, and a workshop building and compound.

New National Headquarters Building Ministry of Social Affairs and Labour, Sultanate of Oman

The winning design in an architectural competition. Designed for a prominent site in the new "Diplomatic City" at Al Khuwair, near Muscat, in the Sultanate of Oman, this new Headquarters Building features a structural frame of reinforced concrete projecting 2m from the external face of the building. This has given opportunity not only of providing a highly modelled exterior, but also introducing additional solar shielding to the main glazed areas.

Laboratories for the Ministry of Commerce and Industry Directorate General for Specifications and Measurements, Ruwi, Muscat, Oman
Above   a general exterior view showing the building in its characteristically mountainous Oman setting.
Below left   the main entrance area.

The Main Post Office, Muscat, Oman
One of the initial projects to be undertaken in Muscat following the discovery of oil. The two-storey building was the first main post office in the Sultanate of Oman.

Government Buildings, the Sultanate of Oman

Above Administrative Offices; sun-shading on a south-facing elevation by projecting access galleries and roof, faced with vertically ribbed precast concrete panels.

Below external view of an ablutions building, showing the modern version of a traditional 'wind-tower' used for ventilation purposes.

Below right an interior view of the 'wind-tower' ventilators.

The Chancery British Embassy, Abu Dhabi; two views of this two-storey building in a garden setting in the main Embassy Compound.

Above **The British Ambassador's Residence, Abu Dhabi;** the Residence is sited within the main Embassy Compound, overlooking the Corniche and the sea. The main reception rooms raised above ground level to provide views across the Arabian Gulf.

Below **Majlis, Saudi Arabia;** the design includes a large shaded reception terrace giving access to the majlis, and thus to the dining room. Both majlis and dining room are 14m square on plan and of the same pyramidal form. It is intended that the majlis will form the initial building of an overall palace development.

Ministry of Public Health Building Project, Doha, Qatar
A limited international competition design for the Ministry's new Headquarters Building on a site in the new West Bay district of Doha.

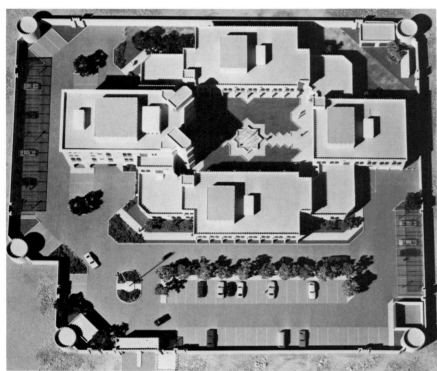

The New National Headquarters for the Development Council of Oman, Al Khuwair, Oman
An appointment made through the Design Competition, this new government building is situated in the new 'Diplomatic City' in the expanding district of Al Khuwair, some 20 km from Muscat.

The Ministry of Agriculture and Fisheries Headquarters Building Project, Muscat, Oman.

The Royal Marine Reserve Headquarters, Bermondsey, London
The general-purpose training and games hall; and the small-bore rifle range.

Characteristic brick elevational designing of a new prison in the UK.

Educational

Al Itehad School, Dubai

Al Itehad School is a private, multi-racial non-profit making organisation. The master plan for the school site proposes a total of four related schools: infants, junior, middle and senior. The design for the Infant's School, as illustrated, was carried out as the main part of a first phase.

The need for protection from the climate, both inside the building and for adjacent open air teaching spaces, combined with the client's request for a single-storey design, resulted in the strongly modelled architectural forms. Maximum shading is provided for windows and the external areas.

The external roof shapes, which are weatherproofed with Du Pont 'Hypalon', are illustrated as dramatically exposed to the sun.

View at ground level of the school, showing sun-shading around the perimeter of the building.

Educational

The John R. Harris Group has been responsible for a variety of educational buildings and related teaching facilities, for private clients and government agencies, both in the United Kingdom and overseas. This work includes a number of new schools designed for both general teaching and specialist educational requirements; and also the renovation and extension of schools. Related teaching facilities in other building types include lecture theatres in health buildings and government training centres. In addition, commercial developments have included full conference facilities.

Left Al Itehad School, Dubai, one of the classrooms, showing the timber roof construction which provides an attractive ceiling.

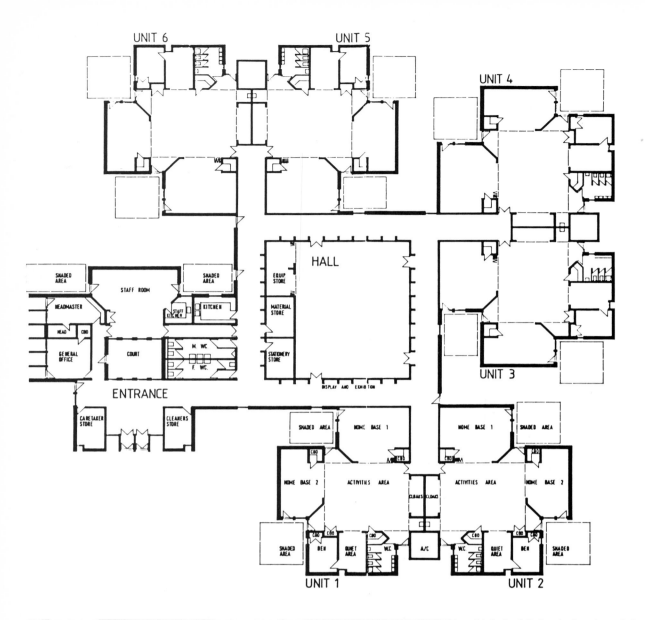

UNIT 6 UNIT 5

UNIT 4

HALL

EQUIP STORE

MATERIAL STORE

STATIONERY STORE

SHADED AREA

STAFF ROOM

SHADED AREA

HEADMASTER

STAFF KITCHEN

KITCHEN

HEAD

CBO

GENERAL OFFICE

COURT

M. WC.

F. WC.

ENTRANCE

CARETAKER STORE

CLEANERS STORE

DISPLAY AND EXHIBITION

UNIT 3

SHADED AREA HOME BASE 1

HOME BASE 1 SHADED AREA

CBO

CBO

CBO

HOME BASE 2 ACTIVITIES AREA

ACTIVITIES AREA HOME BASE 2

CLOAKS CLOAKS

CBO CBO

CBO

CBO CBO

SHADED AREA

DEN QUIET AREA

W.C.

A/C

W.C.

QUIET AREA DEN

SHADED AREA

UNIT 1 UNIT 2

Al Itehad School; the plan of the Infant's School. Each of the four schools proposed for the site is designed as a 'village', providing a range of linked internal and shaded external spaces.
Left the hall, illustrating the use of controlled natural top-lighting.

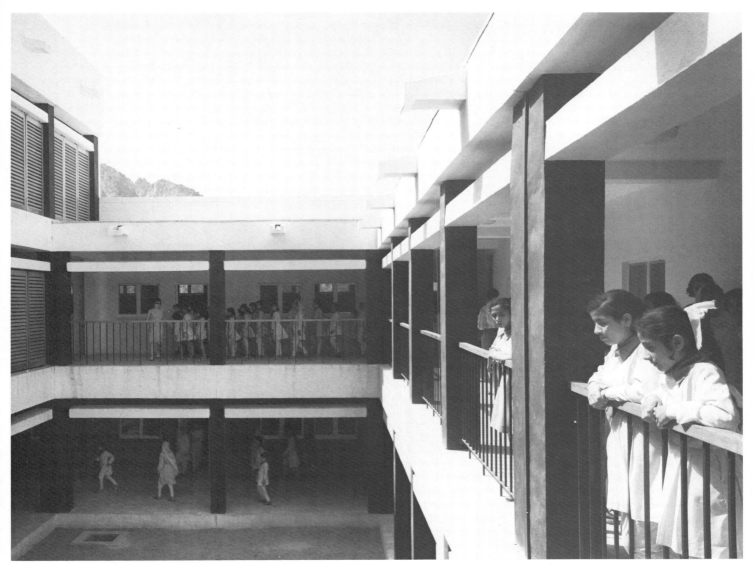

Girls School, Muscat, Oman

The first girls school to be established in Oman. A court-yard plan was adopted in order to ensure privacy from outside the site, and also to enable the shaded open air verandahs and corridors to be accessible from the teaching areas. The accommodation includes general and specialist classrooms, an assembly hall, and staff residential accommodation.

Above   the shaded courtyard of the school
Below   the southern elevation, showing the sun-shading of classroom windows.

The English-Speaking School, Muscat, Oman
The school provides twelve classrooms for 300 children; a library, administrative department and staff housing. The buildings are sited on an east-west axis, giving long elevations to the north and south in order to minimise solar heat gain.

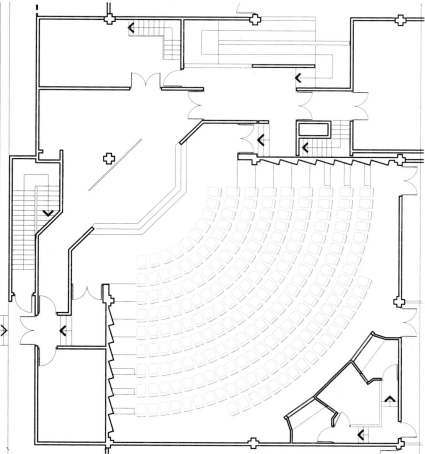

The computer generated plan of a lecture theatre in a health services administration building.

A lecture theatre in the
Dubai Hospital.

**Wellesley House and
St Peter's Court
School, Kent**
The new assembly hall
of Wellesley House
School, incorporating
the old chapel of St
Peter's Court School,
which was re-erected on
the new site (see also
overpage).

School, Alconbury, UK

A split level design of linked blocks related to the natural sloping contours of the site. Facilities include general purpose classrooms, library, rooms for science, biology, economics and music, and a multi-purpose assembly hall with provision for physical education.

Above stairway bridge access to the second of three floors of the main teaching block.
Left a music practice room.

94

School, Lakenheath, UK
The school forms part of the development programme for the expansion of educational facilities for the families of air force personnel. Accommodation provided includes classrooms, a multi-purpose assembly hall and gymnasium, and full catering facilities.

Wellesley House and St Peter's Court School, Kent
The firm has added a new residential house, assembly hall and classrooms to the original school, shown on the left of the photograph above; and the design has been prepared for an activities/sports hall, with art and music centres, as the perspective drawing on the left.

Residential

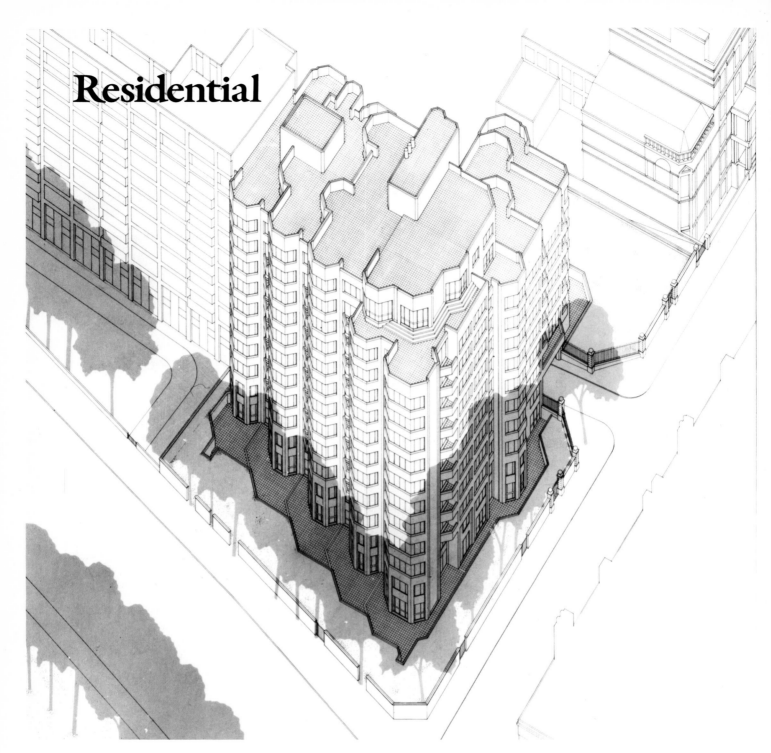

Residential

Residential buildings have been designed by The John R. Harris Group for both private clients, government agencies and commercial clients, in the United Kingdom and widely overseas. Work in the private sector includes individual residences, housing estate development and multi-storey apartments. Public sector work includes Ambassador's Residences for the United Kingdom, and the United States of America, also staff residential accommodation for hospitals and industrial developments; and barracks and single-person and married family quarters for defence projects.

Thorney Court Apartments, Palace Gate, London

A 12-storey building containing a total of sixty luxury apartments, facing the Royal Palace of Kensington and the Gardens. The distinctive 'bay-window' modelling was adopted in order to take maximum advantage of the magnificent panoramic views across the Royal Parks, and to provide a pleasingly scaled appearance when viewed from the Gardens. This elevational motif also echoes the historic bay-windows along Park Lane.

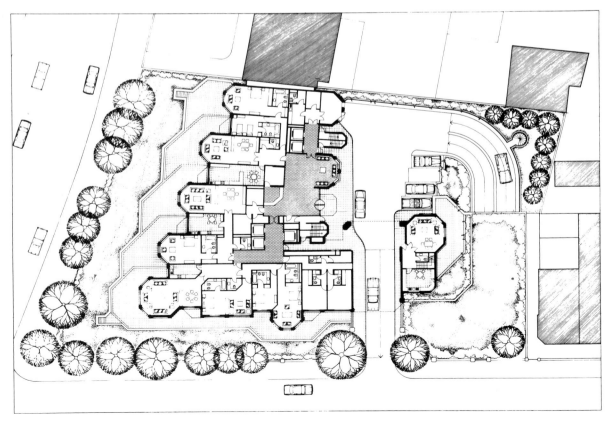

Thorney Court seen beyond Broad Walk and the trees of Kensington Palace Gardens; and the ground floor plan.

Thorney Court Apartments; the south-facing elevation, showing the balconies created by the stepped building form; and a typical kitchen dining area.

Mixed Development, Worthing, England
There are three floors of apartments, over ground level
retail space, with pedestrian access from Marine Parade
and vehicular access from the adjoining multi-storey car
park. Each apartment has a generous south or west
facing balcony, to take advantage of the magnificent
seafront views.

Left Templemead, a detail view of this single-storey house in the orchard garden of an Edwardian house (see also page 28).

Below and *right* a basement swimming pool and adjoining sitting area and bar, for a luxury apartment in London.

Private houses.
Left Swain's Wood; *Right* Chenestone.

On the building signage:

مركز دبي التجاري الدولي
duba international trade centre

الشقق المفروشة
the apartments

Far left **The Dubai International Trade Centre;** one of the 15-storey residential buildings which together provide a total of 492 luxury furnished apartments.

Left **Three-storey bachelor flats for the Government of Oman;** the shaded corner balconies are enclosed by louvre shutters.

Below **Defence accommodation in Oman,** the perforated concrete blocks used for the access balcony and at roof level encourage ventilation and minimise heat build-up.

The American Ambassador's Residence, Abu Dhabi.

Banker's Residence, Dubai.

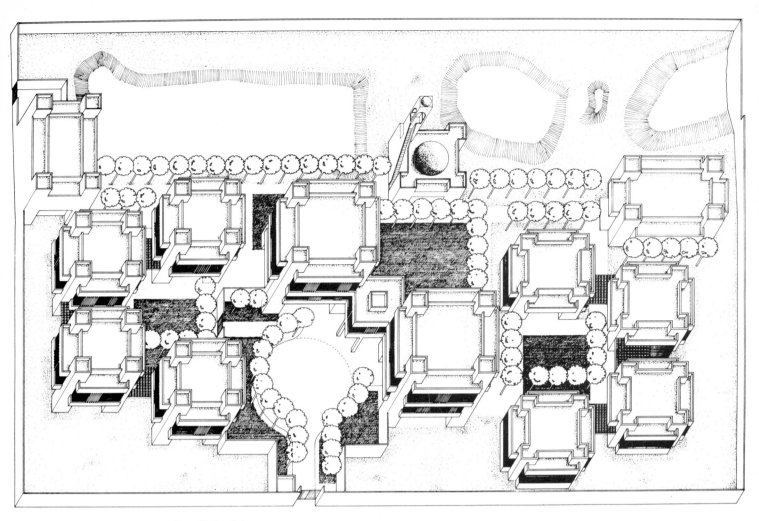

Apartments Development, Saudi Arabia.

Housing in Negara Brunei Darussalam
Top single-storey houses for staff of the Royal Brunei Polo Club;
Left two-storey senior staff houses.

Oil Company Residential Accommodation, Abu Dhabi.

Oil company staff residential accommodation, Oman

Housing, Qurum, capital area of Oman

Planning

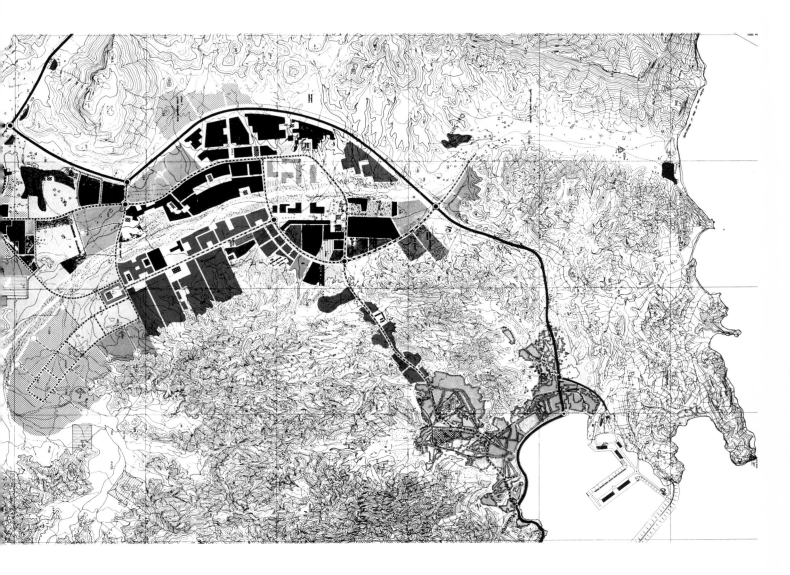

Development Plan, Greater Mutrah, Oman

Mutrah, and nearby Muscat itself, are the two original
historic nucleii of the greatly enlarged modern capital
city of Oman. Following the discovery and commercial
production of oil in the country, John R Harris Architects were commissioned to update their earlier Development Plan for Mutrah and to prepare a detailed plan and
report for the extensive enlargement of the existing main
urban area to provide for an envisaged increase in population.

The new plan proposed the infrastructure for a new
town extending from Mutrah into the adjacent valley. It
also identified areas for immediate development and for
future expansion.

Left   the new Corniche along the bay at Mutrah, for
which the firm were consultant architects and town
planners; and a view of the old waterfront, when direct
access from one end of Mutrah to the other was only
possible along the beach at low tide.

Above   the Master Plan for Greater Mutrah; the old
town area at the head of the bay, and the new deepwater
facilities of Port Qaboos at the bottom right.

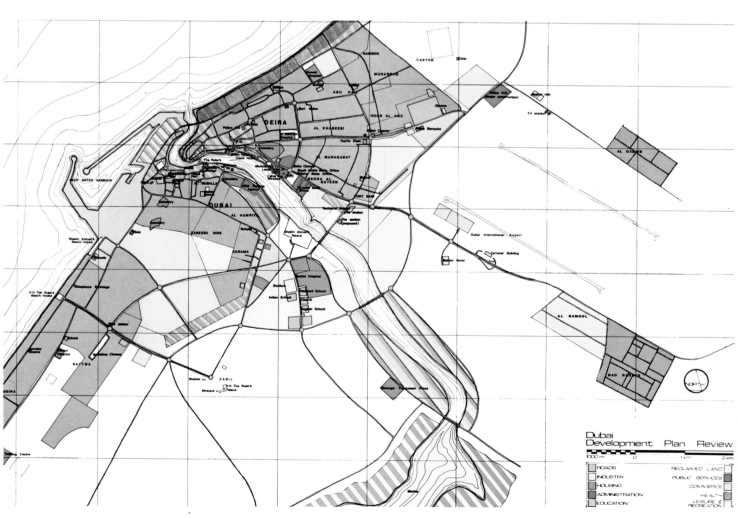

Dubai
Development Plan Review

ROADS
INDUSTRY
HOUSING
ADMINISTRATION
EDUCATION

RECLAIMED LAND
PUBLIC SERVICES
COMMERCE
HEALTH
LEISURE &
RECREATION

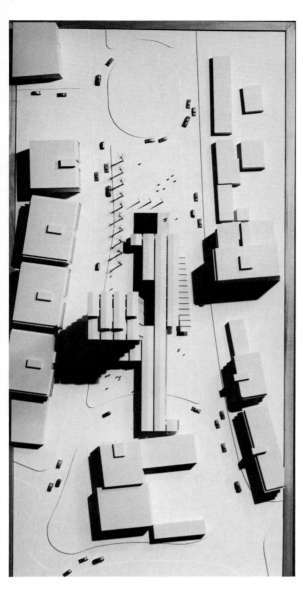

Development Plan for Dubai, UAE
John R Harris Architects were responsible in 1971 for a major review of their original town plan for Dubai, which had been prepared more than a decade earlier. Since the first plan was published there had been extensive development in Dubai, including the completion of a large deepwater harbour and the international airport. Analysis of the growth pattern of development enabled predictions for future expansion to be made. Further major developments include the construction of a road tunnel under the Creek, widening of the original bridge, and construction of a second major bridge which forms part of the regional UAE motorway network, linking Abu Dhabi with Ras al Khaimah.

The aerial photograph shows the city in the late 1950s, looking across Dubai, on the western bank of the Creek, to Deira.

Dubai Central Area
A design for a new commercial complex, providing facilities for offices, restaurants, and a shopping precinct, linked by a system of pedestrian walkways.

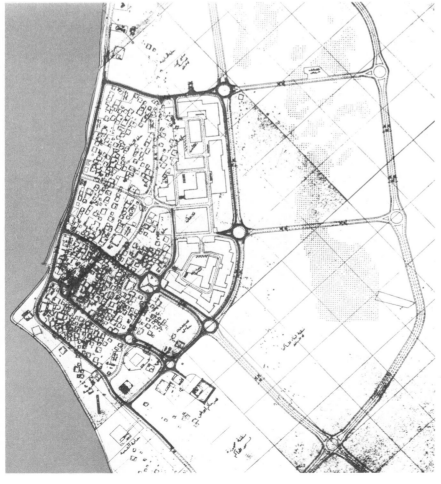

City of Abu Dhabi, Survey and Development Plan
After discovery of oil in commercial quantities, John R Harris was appointed by the Government of Abu Dhabi to prepare a comprehensive development plan and report. The plan has formed the basis of the City's dramatic development through to the present day

Zhuhai Special Economic Zone of the People's Republic of China

The Master Plan report was formulated by a consortium of international consultants. The development brief was to define the broad land-use inter-relationships of the Master Plan and to indicate the framework of physical structure planning. The plan area has a coastline length of 16km and the total land area for development is 10km².

There are five basic elements identified in the Master Plan:

- a new town for a working population of 100,000 persons, designed to international standards and incorporating the latest concepts of urban development;
- a leisure and recreation resort area centred on an 18-hole golf course and a public park and yacht marina;
- an industrial workers housing and technical training area;
- a 200 hectare 'industrial park' based on industries using advanced technologies;
- the appraisal and integration into the Master Plan of an existing residential and mixed-uses zone.

The Master Plan is open-ended and allows for controlled growth of each of the major components of the plan.

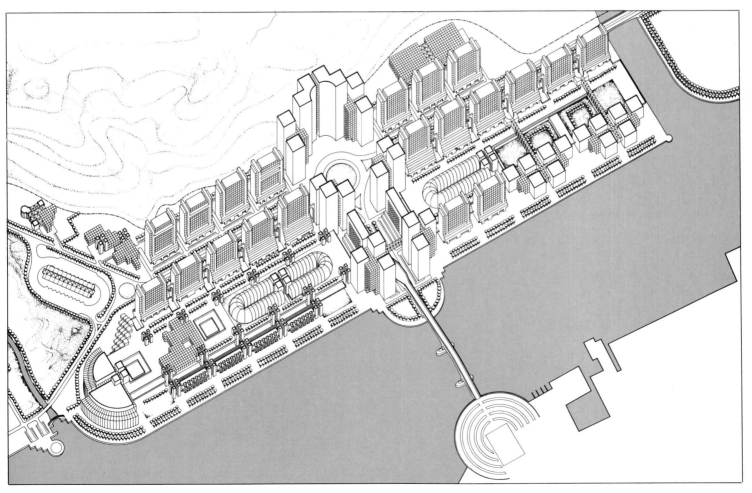

Leisure

Sports Stadium, Dubai
The design of the Dubai sports complex provides for comprehensive games facilities to Olympic standards.

Al Baha Sports Centre, Saudi Arabia
The club house, left; and the theatre, below.

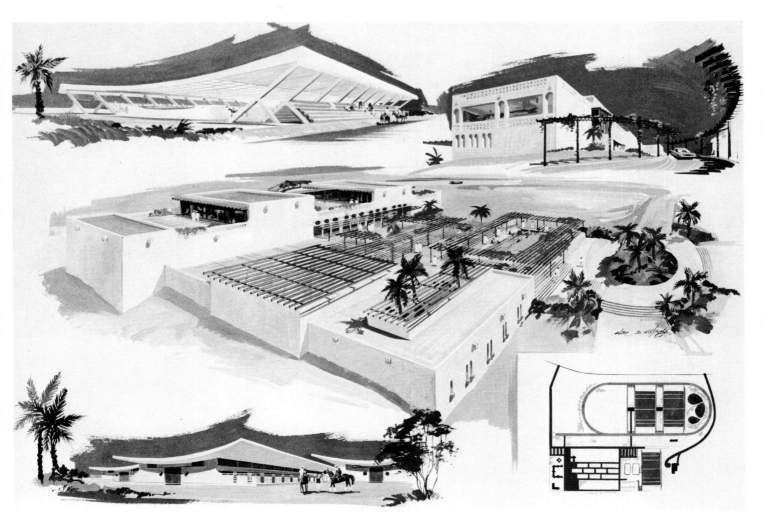

Polo ground and club facilities, Sharjah.

Left **The Royal Jeru-dong Polo Club, Negara Brunei Darussalam;** top an international invitation match in progress.
Below the main clubhouse and swimming pool.
This page, five views of the **Brunei Shell Recreation Club, Seria, Negara Brunei Darussalam.**

A personal postscript: John R. Harris

The book covers the period of development in Europe and other parts of the world, after the devastation of World War II. The rapid expansion of communications, especially of air travel, after the War dramatically affected the scope of work from a London base. The book illustrates a broad range of planning projects and buildings designated by the practices in many differing climatic conditions.

No man is an island.
The schemes illustrated and described are the creative work of many people: clients, consultants, builders, colleagues, good friends in many places, and my wife Jill to whom I owe so much and might never have met if it had not been for the Architectural Association.
I remember three great men I have had the good fortune to know. Their names and those of many others who have been an inspiration remain unmentioned.

Architecture is an art, it has no beginning and no end. Wisdom in design surely lives in love and harmony with nature, but unity coupled with regional diversity is the true fundamental character of great art.

John R. Harris

Partners and some members of the office of the John R Harris group who have contributed to its achievements:

Stuart Aston
Ian Bampton
Michael Blyth
Christopher Broad-Manges
Colin Brown
Christopher Capewell
Michael Choy
Geoffrey Cooper
Stuart Davis
David Dunstan
Edmund Emamooden
Stephen Finch
Michael Foster
Brian Frankcombe
Kenneth Gibbs
Keith Grantham
Roger Gridley
Victor Hadman
George Hall
Mark Harris
Gordon Heald
Alan Hendon
Anthony Hickman
Anthony Hill
Michael Houghton
Peter Jackson
Melvyn John
Alan Jones
Edouard Koenig
John Lane
Stephen Lee
Victor Lim
Anthony Lodge
Brian MacFarlane
Colin McNab
Andrew Major
Brian Mihlenstedt
Christopher Mitchell
Harold Pugh
Jim Pyrke
Hal Smith
James Smith
Christopher Stevens
Peter Vincent
Jeffrey Wall
James Williams
Derrick Wolf
Marc Zihler

The opening of the Dubai International Trade Centre by Her Majesty the Queen and His Highness Sheikh Rashid Ibn Said Al-Maktoum.

Zhuhai

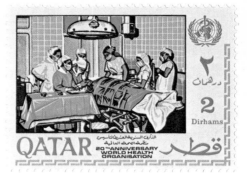

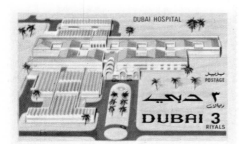

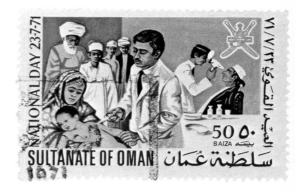

Commemorative stamps and banknote illustrating buildings
designed by the John R Harris group.